LUCIDITY IN SPORTS

LUCIDITY
IN SPORTS

GET CLARITY OF MIND
WHEN UNDER PRESSURE

STEPHANIE CUNHA, Ph.D.
LISA D LUCCHESI, M.S.

MENTAL
ACCELERATOR.

Published by Mental Accelerator

Portland, Oregon

www.mentalaccelerator.com

Cover design by Stephanie Cunha.

Cover image credit: Vectorfusionart/Shutterstock.

Library of Congress Control Number: 2021902647

Print ISBN: 978-1-7346615-3-8

eBook ISBN: 978-1-7346615-4-5

Hardcover ISBN: 978-1-7346615-6-9

Printed in the United States of America on acid-free paper.

First Edition

This book is for those who continuously seek to improve.

CONTENTS

INTRODUCTION

WHAT IS LUCIDITY AND WHAT DOES IT MEAN TO BE LUCID?

*****

"I felt a strange calmness…a kind of euphoria. I felt I could run all day without tiring, dribble through any of their team or all of them, and almost pass through them physically. I felt I could not be hurt. It was a bizarre feeling; one I had not felt before. Perhaps it was merely confidence, but I have often felt confident without that strange feeling of invincibility."

These words, describing a mental state of clear lucidity, were written by soccer legend Pelé in a 2006 biography. This particular state is a fundamental element of what is known as "being in the zone" or the flow state. But what is it concretely?

> To be lucid, a person directly interacts with their environment and is immersed in the present moment and actions. The state of lucidity involves ongoing action that calls for discernment, the correctness of perception, decision, and action of the individual. It requires immediate feedback, which validates the gesture successfully. Most importantly, the attention is focused on the task rather than oneself. You do not observe yourself; you are immersed in what you do.

The state of lucidity requires full availability of body and mind. As a result, the activity of the prefrontal cortex decreases, which ends internal chatter and planning logic. The individual is no longer in a state of "wanting to do" but is now "letting it be." Intuition takes precedence over rationality, such as in the state of flow.

This trance state is explained by several chemical discharges released in the brain, including serotonin, dopamine, and leptin. In response to a person's feeling of total disconnection when involved in the flow process, Mihaly Csíkszentmihályi, a psychologist famous for his investigations on the concept of flow, explains that the nervous system is unable to process more than one hundred ten bits of information per second. For comparison, our brains process sixty bits per second during a conversation, so it is difficult—if not impossible—to listen to two people talking simultaneously. When a person is in a flow state and has total lucidity, their brain processes about a hundred bits of information per second, leaving the nervous system with insufficient room to pay attention to the rest.

The state of lucidity is not specific to sport. While it finds its natural expression through the characteristics of athletics—performance, physical skills, technical skills, and mental and emotional management—it is present elsewhere: in our professional life, public speaking, and leisure activities such as music and reading. It can also occur in simple moments like while playing with children, a debate between friends, or a hike with family. The psychologist Daniel Goleman then speaks of "fluidity" that almost everyone knows occasionally, which is when you give your best and go beyond your limits.

> Lucidity can be defined as seeing and understanding a situation clearly and accurately. It calls upon qualities of discernment and emotional stability. Lucidity is the ability to step back and consider all possibilities when facing a critical situation.

Becoming lucid is a process of leveling up to the next state of awareness, where your ability to directly know, perceive, feel, or be cognizant of events is multiplied. Lucidity is essential for reacting to pressure, stress, and emotion. It contributes to the athlete's resilience and ability to strategize and make quick decisions amid uncertainty. Lucidity is essential in staying a step ahead of one's opponent.

NO LUCIDITY WITHOUT...

*****

- Motivation and determination
- Capacity for analysis and judgment
- Emotional stability
- Sense of responsibility
- Insight
- Clairvoyance
- Sense of reality
- Physical and mental resistance
- Humility (knowing yourself and your limits)
- Training and mastery of skills

"Lucidity is the fruit of the mobilization of knowledge and judgment, strategic reasoning, the fruit of a vision for the future, a synthesis exercise; it should not be confused with the flash of genius expected like an oracle by certain decision-makers…lucidity is forged by experience…lucidity is educated."

—Daniel Hervouët, *Mener des hommes vers le succès* (2014).

INTERVIEW WITH A PROFESSIONAL
SNOWBOARDER ABOUT LUCIDITY

*****

Paul Henri Delerue is a retired snowboarder with an impressive track record: Junior World Champion in 2004, Olympic bronze medalist in 2006, and fourth at the Sochi Games 2014. (This interview was translated from leadershipducoeur.com)

What is lucidity for you?

For me, a lucid person is, above all, lucid about themselves: their strengths, weaknesses, goals, the way to reach their goals, and the energy they want to devote to them. It is just as much about their environment: the threats, the opportunities, the snow, the weather, the opponents, the context, the challenges…. Their strategy is clear and achievable. They remain faithful to their strategy while being attentive to the situation.

Have you ever lacked lucidity?

I was bold and determined very often, especially at the start of my athletic career. Over the years, my experience has led me to more caution and control because I've become more lucid. The more I moved forward, the more stable my benchmarks were and the more reliable my decision-making was.

My most significant lack of lucidity was during the Vancouver Olympics in 2010. I was twenty-six years old. When I didn't think I was stressed on the first turn, I failed to lower my center of gravity enough to provide a good turn. In other words, a stress ball in my belly cut the connection between my brain and my legs so that I couldn't bend them enough. When the proprioceptive information came from my feet to my head, this feeling was so unusual that I thought my board was broken. As a result, I spent the whole of my descent on the defensive, afraid of making mistakes, instead of attacking and looking for the pleasure of snowboarding. The stress then completely altered my vision of reality. I finished twenty-fifth, a massive failure for me.

This lack of lucidity is due to two significant errors during my preparation. First, I could not identify my fear of losing my status as an Olympic medalist. I was the only French snowboard medalist at the Turin Games in 2006. This fear refers to my fear of no longer existing, the fear of dying symbolically. When that fear came to me on that day, I couldn't identify it, let alone control it.

Also, I knew I would be stressed on race day. Instead of implementing psychological, physiological, and behavioral strategies, I decided to deny this state of tension. The boomerang effect was highly violent!

That day, the stress that I had tried not to see completely took control of my perception of reality. I've never been so not lucid in my life. Today, I am convinced that suppressing or denying your emotions is only a way to escape, not a strategy!

How do you keep a clear mind in difficult times?

There are different ways to stay in control of adversity. They are all linked. First, I like to see the opportunity before the threat. This is how I put my intention. How is this situation challenging for me? I like challenges and always wanted to make sense of my goals.

Since there is a stake, there is stress. It's up to me to make this stress an engine rather than a brake! Whenever I feel this famous belly ball fall into place, I focus on my breathing first. I breathe in five seconds through my nose and breathe out five seconds through my mouth while standing straight. While breathing like this, I focus on my body's tension. I feel the tensions evolve in my body, and I feel them gradually disappear. We are then in the physiological approach since I eliminate in this way a significant amount of cortisol, the stress hormone. I am at the same time in the psychological approach since it allows me to eliminate my parasitic thoughts. I'm only with myself. There is no more stake, no more pressure. Only myself, in accordance with my body. Five minutes later, when I opened my eyes again, my parasitic thoughts disappeared. My mind is serene. My priority objective is clear. I know what I must do because, during my preparation, I anticipated the problems I might encounter during the race. I know them by heart. I trust myself. My eyes are now wide open. I am in harmony with my environment. The starter shouts, "Riders ready, five seconds, ready! GO!"

I'm in the race. I know precisely all the most strategic places in my race: where to be and where not to be. I know my opponents. I am a master of my board, journey, and myself. I know the unthinkable can happen. In any case, I will react white or black. This is my behavioral approach: I don't know gray. Each behavior is determined. I do things two hundred percent. I am here and now, giving the best of myself, playing, having fun, and living my childhood dream: I am becoming an Olympic medalist.

SECTION 1 WHAT LOSING LUCIDITY LOOKS LIKE?

BEING TOO SELF-CONSCIOUS: THE SPOTLIGHT EFFECT

*****

Have you ever walked into your event venue and felt your nerves couldn't handle it? Your heart's racing, your breath is short, you're sweating, and you feel like all eyes are on you—even if they're not. These are just some of the many ways that self-consciousness—an individual's knowledge of their thoughts, feelings, and actions—can manifest itself.

Focusing too much on yourself and your feelings isolates yourself from the outside world, likely causing you to lose lucidity. When you're self-conscious, not only do you make your anxiety worse, but you're also less aware of what's going on around you. This can cause you to think that other people are judging you negatively; in reality, they likely aren't paying attention at all. Psychologists have given a name to this phenomenon: the spotlight effect.

The spotlight effect comes from being overly self-conscious and unable to see the other person's perspective—it's almost surely much different than yours! The spotlight effect is a cognitive bias that causes people to overestimate the degree to which they are observed and noticed by others and the degree to which others care about the things they notice about them. The spotlight effect can strongly influence your thinking in various situations, so it's important to understand it.

With athletes, excessive self-consciousness causes a sort of permanent anxiety about how they're perceived. It's characterized by a fear of blushing or being noticed, not doing the right thing, or not having the right attitude; it's a general lack of confidence. When in the throes of self-consciousness, it's nearly impossible to remember how to stop feeling that way and accurately assess situations. It causes people to choke during competition. Perhaps most affected by self-consciousness are athletes in individual sports of timing and precision, such as gymnastics, diving, and golf. Conversely, in sports that mostly require sheer effort and force of will—running and weightlifting, for example—self-consciousness is less likely to sabotage performance.

To avoid self-consciousness, you must develop an outward focus and learn perspective. That's why preparing ahead of time is so important, which is usually when you feel ready to tackle the problem instead of succumbing to it.

NERVE-WRACKING STAGE FRIGHT

*****

Stage fright is a natural reflex by which our brain reacts to a situation interpreted as danger. It can also be defined as unreasonable anxiety when approaching an important event such as an interview, a stage performance, an audition, or a competition. Our body responds with a series of physiological manifestations, which are supposed to protect us or allow us to defend ourselves: tremors, sweaty hands, blurred vision, dry mouth, and stiff limbs. Do you know, for example, that perspiration on the hands allowed us to better hang on trees while fleeing a predator? During evolution, this one-time survival mechanism is now associated with psychological stress.

Analyze the manifestations of stage fright and anxiety-provoking situations so that you know what to work on. Make a list and try to understand when and how they affect your performance. Do you suffer from physiological effects, like famous singers Barbara Streisand and Rod Stewart, whose anxiety causes them to vomit just before going on stage? Or do you have psychological manifestations, like memory lapses, which have long been a problem for several actors like Hugh Grant and Laurence Olivier? Doing this will allow you to adopt the best method for controlling your stage fright, and the possibilities are numerous: meditation, psychoanalysis, and homeopathy, to name a few. Everyone is different, and no miracle recipe exists to alleviate stage fright.

You should work on eliminating stage fright during preparation and behind the scenes just before going on stage and during the performance. You can learn how to manage your stage fright. Set long-term goals, and take every opportunity to perform in public, which will get you closer to vanquishing—or at least controlling— stage fright.

Stage fright is a response to stress that gives us the vigilance and the energy mobilization necessary to perform at the highest possible level. However, everyone feels a different point of resistance to stage fright; in extreme cases, an athlete or performer may be unable to overcome it and must retire.

Some people use medication such as anxiolytics and beta-blockers to reduce the effects of stage fright. The most commonly used drugs block stress reactions and are generally used to treat high blood pressure or cardiac arrhythmias. Their use for better performance is controversial, as they quickly become a crutch that appears to help face fears but serves to avoid the problem.

Several harmless ways to reduce stage fright include practicing relaxation and breathing techniques before stressful events. Set realistic goals, prepare well, and rehearse in front of a small audience. Finally, visualize the event and your ability to perform well.

FORGETTING INFORMATION IN THE MOMENT

*****

> The aforementioned memory lapses that actors sometimes experience are called procedural memory malfunction due to loss of lucidity.

Perhaps you've seen the video of director Michael Bay at a Samsung press conference in 2014. We see Bay, director of many American blockbusters, appear on stage during a presentation of a new Samsung television. After a few words, the director becomes confused, tries to catch himself, then stops talking. The interviewer, hoping to help, asks him a question but receives no response. Bay then turns on his heels and leaves the stage.

You may find yourself lost during a presentation, a competition, or a performance.

How can panic be managed if it occurs despite preparation? How can it be overcome to avoid the flight reflex?

In theater, this panic is called a "hole."

> Those who have experienced it know it's not just a memory lapse. If only for a fraction of a second, your attention is distracted, and suddenly, you feel like your brain is blacking out—like you have no idea what you're doing. Panic happens when you feel that the audience realizes you're lost. Your embarrassment amplifies the stress, and you enter the vicious circle Michael Bay experienced. This has happened to many competitors and performers.

I was attending a black belt grading in a karate seminar. One student performed well, but it was time for a spectacular jump. All eyes were on him.

And…he did it perfectly! I could see his face relax. His focus was totally on the execution of that jump. And he made it successfully. But then I saw his face go from relaxation and satisfaction to doubt, fear, and panic. He couldn't remember the next move. He was standing in the middle of the mats, unsure what to do next. Desperate, he started to do uncoordinated movements in the wrong sequence.

He knew the moves were wrong but preferred to do something instead of just standing there. He had just experienced a hole and failed his black belt grading.

Out of the hole

Regaining control is the goal while in a hole. There's no point in exhausting yourself by straining your memory. The more you search, the less of a chance it'll return. In the case of a speech, you use your memory sequentially: one sentence leads to another, and in most cases, everything goes well. But sometimes, this logical thread can break. Fortunately, there is another way to access memory: perceptions.

We've all had memories come back after smelling, touching, or seeing something. If you find yourself in a hole, take a deep breath, stay calm, and disconnect from your audience. Look for anything that can remind you of the work accomplished: a computer on which you worked until exhaustion, a worn-out remote control, an annotated file—this is where your preparation will pay off: The more you've repeated, the more each object will bring you back to the thread of your talk.

You'll have a hole sooner or later if you speak to audiences regularly. Do not fear it. Instead, wait for it and apply this method. You'll see that the thread of your words will suddenly fall back into place.

Some time ago, I accompanied a colleague to a seminar. A few minutes before her scheduled presentation, she began to imagine everything that could go wrong. I told her, "Don't worry, you're going to stay an hour on stage, and there will inevitably be a few distractions." She laughed and stopped talking about what could go wrong. She had a memory lapse during the conference but quickly found a way out. In the end, I asked her if she'd been upset, and she replied, "No, I remembered that you warned me that it would happen, so I managed."

LOSING THE CAPABILITY TO THINK CLEARLY

*****

Let's take a soccer game as an example. The physical aspect of the sport, already challenging, is only a small part of what it takes to be successful.

During a game, the ball's different trajectories, the teammates' continual movement, and the opponent's effort threaten a player's achievement.

The realization of a technical sequence results from processing information that requires the player to analyze and structure the data from the environment, their knowledge of the game, and their own body to develop an answer and control it.

The components for this are:

• Perceptual skills: Being able to read the game and process the information;

• Knowledge: Mastering the principles and rules of the game;

• Analytical skills: A player must be able to link what they know and see when immersed in a game situation. They are closely correlated with their memorization abilities and reasoning skills;

• Decision-making skills: Making the right choice in the shortest possible time;

• The capacities of action that will allow the player to execute the appropriate technique. Confidence, at this stage of the sequence, is primordial.

To summarize, athletes need to think quickly. Information cannot pass directly from the external environment to our internal black box without passing through the short-term memory. The short-term memory allows you to keep information for a few seconds, no more. This memory is sensitive to anxiety and distractions. Losing lucidity will translate to a drastic decrease in short-term memory capabilities, resulting in an inability to respond appropriately.

SHOWING HESITATION

*****

Hesitation is a liability in almost every sport. External pressure or internal traits such as fear of failure or making the wrong decision may cause hesitation. When you lose lucidity, you lose the capability to think clearly and analyze the whole situation, which is crucial to making decisions. Thus, hesitation follows, which can be devastating in sports: Hesitant basketball players get shots blocked, and quarterbacks hesitate and get intercepted.

Hesitation can also be a problem for extreme sport athletes, a group known as risk-takers. Knowing how to manage fear is essential to progress in your practice—which is easier said than done.

When a skateboarder begins to skate, the notion of risk is theoretical. Then come the first falls as they increase the complexity of their routines. Then come the injuries.

From the first fall, our brain goes into reaction and protection mode: falling hurts, and I don't want to drop anymore. I must not try this because I could fall. This theoretical fear becomes concrete and associated with painful memories, and our brain constructs unpleasant projections of what could happen. This process is quite normal, and it helps protect us.

But to the skateboarder, it's harmful because it leads to behaviors such as these, which can hinder their performance:

• Blockages about certain tricks;

• Hesitation: They want to do a trick but can't. Sometimes, they start hesitantly, which induces muscle tension, stiffness instead of fluidity, and, consequently, a fall;

• Increased fear and the creation of a myth around some tricks.

Committing to the execution of your next movement will prevent hesitation. But remember that you should always know your limits and abilities. There's a big difference between committing to a trick within your reach and one that isn't.

What characterizes the best skaters is their ability to deal with fear. Knowing that a trick is potentially dangerous doesn't stop confident skateboarders from doing it—as long as they've thoroughly prepared. And only when the trick is attempted with complete confidence and lucidity is success possible. So, no hesitation!

Another example is combat sports.

Along with not hesitating, there should be a steadfast willingness to take action. Commitment. It's what leads to success. Competition isn't a place to experiment; it isn't a place to hesitate or to observe, but rather, it is a place to test your practiced techniques, see them in action, and see what works and what doesn't. If you're hesitating, you likely don't believe in your technique and don't have lucidity. Hesitation results from training in a way that doesn't encourage action—so change how you train if this happens to you.

The more you drill, the more your body becomes attuned to specific movements, actions, and reactions. If you've drilled 10,000 times to do a leg swipe after the opponent tries a roundhouse kick on you, chances are that your counterattack will be smooth and automatic when an opponent tries on.

Anyone who trains should aim for this: reactions should be automatic without hesitation. Otherwise, they are likely to fail.

Here's an example of hesitation affecting an athlete: On the Sachsenring motorsport racing circuit, Fabio Quartararo started from the front row and struggled to pass Marc Marquez at the first corner. Jostled by Jack Miller, he struggled in the leading group until the start of the second round.

"I made a mistake," Quartararo said. "I wanted to pass Petrucci, but at that point, I was hesitant to go; it was unclear. I made the wrong decision." Too quick on the corner, he lost control of his moto.

It was the first time he hadn't finished a race in MotoGP due to hesitation.

BECOMING PARALYZED BY OVERANALYSIS

*****

"Movement is life" is a Navy SEAL expression reminding its members not to freeze when attacked.

Do you know the paradox of Buridan's donkey? It's this:

A donkey stood before a peck of oats and a bucket of water. He didn't know where to start. He spends so much time thinking about and wondering which would be the best choice that he ends up starving and thirsty.

This absurd example perfectly illustrates what paralysis of analysis is.

What is paralysis of analysis?

Analysis paralysis, or analytical paralysis, happens when you overanalyze things. It is when we fail to make decisions because we are afraid of making the wrong choice and/or because we face too many options.

Instead of deciding and acting, we get stuck in the research-and-reflection phase, evaluating and studying our options, weighing the pros and cons—without taking action. Doing research is healthy in itself. It allows us to make informed decisions. However, it becomes a problem when this research phase drags on and becomes an excuse to delay our choices.

The consequences of paralysis of analysis

Paralysis of analysis is problematic on several levels.

First, it decreases our mental performance. When you're paralyzed by analysis, you feel stressed and anxious, which causes a lack of concentration. It also harms our creativity. Stanford University professor Grace Hawthorne says that thinking too hard prevents us from presenting our most creative work. Many of us have experienced this as writer's block. Ideas are jostling in our heads, and we don't know where to start. This "white-page syndrome" is nothing more than a form of paralysis of analysis.

Studies show that overthinking causes us to choke under pressure. Analysis paralysis is an anti-pattern, a typical response to a recurring problem that is ineffective. It is a state in which we freeze or pause, even for a millisecond, during an activity that ultimately affects the outcome of the action we're trying to perform.

Let's consider a weightlifter performing a snatch, which requires many minuscule details to do it correctly. Newbies often focus on all these details while trying to accomplish the complex snatch. With so many essential points to focus on, it's easy to succumb to analysis paralysis and fumble the lift.

By overanalyzing, you can quite easily create a self-fulfilling prophecy of failure. We've all heard of beginner's luck, but it's often because they didn't overthink it—they gave it a go!

So, how do you overcome analysis paralysis? Firstly, regular practice will help. Doing complicated movements regularly allows you to focus on problem areas while spending less time on areas you've mastered. Regular practice will give you more muscle memory and enable you to move more naturally. Therefore, less effort is required to think through all the movements as they are meant to happen.

Another great way to defeat analysis paralysis is to focus on only two or three critical points during movement. This will give your mind enough capacity to act on them more effectively, and you can achieve a better result sooner.

Analysis paralysis is real; it can be problematic for many people in various areas. But you'll see improvement by simplifying the situation and attacking areas you need to improve.

ENTERING THE PANIC STATE

*****

From anxiety to panic: how to regain control

I once interviewed a triathlete after a semi-pro race. Her words were telling: "My triathlons are systematically sealed by catastrophic swimming. I am far from being a good swimmer, but I train enough in the pool and the ocean to claim to do a correct swim. But as soon as I am on the starting line with others, I stress and panic so much that I suffocate once in the water, and it is almost impossible for me to swim efficiently. At one point, I nearly called the emergency canoe to bring me back to dry land. I train regularly in the ocean between June and October and swim without a problem. The difference is that I'm alone...

Sunday at the race, on the 500-meter swimming, it was a butcher's shop—I knew it. I went to the outdoors to try to isolate myself as much as possible. Unfortunately, I've panicked from the start. I went out in 18 min, a catastrophe to continue behind. I get angry more because I am pretty good on the bike and running."

When facing the swim portion of a triathlon, several factors may impact your lucidity and cause panic, such as the cold temperature of the water and the number of people entering the water.

When switching from pool training to open water, consider the water conditions and environmental factors affecting swimming.

Cooler water makes the person feel more nervous, more apprehensive, and less comfortable. Not being able to see the bottom can also increase the stress level for a swimmer who is not used to open water. One thing you must master is orientation, which allows you to go in the right direction and helps keep you lucid. You have to lift your head just enough for your eyes to escape the water. If you raise it too high, your hips will settle, and swimming efficiency will be affected. This can be practiced in the pool.

The swimmer must also choose a wetsuit suitable for swimming, which is thicker at the chest and hips and thinner at the shoulders. You will feel compressed, and movement will be more difficult, but you have to get used to it.

The swimmer must avoid panicking, especially when tired from the shore or in cold, deep water. Eventually, they will get used to these conditions. They should train with a partner or ask someone to accompany them by kayak or paddleboard. Just having someone with you in the water can lower stress levels.

If a swimmer makes a distance of 1500 meters in the pool, it does not necessarily mean they can achieve an equivalent distance in open water. The first few times, the distances are shortened, and the swimmers swim along the shore. Don't venture out to sea straight away. You will gain confidence and swim short distances, even if it means going back and forth. You have to progress gradually.

CHOKING UNDER PRESSURE

*****

Choking is defined as performing more poorly than expected and can occur in many different scenarios. The aftermath of competition is often gloomy when the goal has not been reached. Something happened. But what? Underperformance or choking is primarily a matter of subjectivity. And sometimes imponderables. Perhaps you were the victim of particularly unfavorable race conditions, like terrible weather or an unexpectedly tricky course. Maybe you've suffered muscle pain or stomach problems. You have to identify—without looking for excuses—the elements that have upset the overall quality of your effort.

Jean Van de Velde has been a professional golfer since 1987. He is best known to the general public for his incredible defeat at the British Open in 1999. Leading by three strokes in this prestigious competition at the start of the last hole, he collapsed, trying unadvisable shots before losing.

He first hit the fairway on the 17th—the problem was that he was on the 18th hole. Not great, but he could've recovered. But in a magnificent panache, he continues, wanting to reach the green of the 18th directly. This is the beginning of the drama. The ball hits the grandstand and ricochets at an improbable angle, landing in the tall grass. Then his third shot ends up in the stream. The climax is reached when Van de Velde rolls up his pants and goes to feel the water, considering playing his ball there. He decides not to, so a penalty stroke is assessed. And then the bunker.

After losing his lead, he is finally forced to play a three-way playoff with Justin Leonard and Paul Lawrie. He finishes second.

How can an athlete play so well throughout a tournament before choking like that on the last hole? What happened?

A similar event happened in 2016. Jordan Spieth was heading for a second consecutive title at the prestigious Masters Tournament. With nine holes to go and a comfortable five-stroke lead, the victory seemed inevitable for the second-best golfer in the world. But his dream journey turned into an absolute nightmare within half an hour.

During the 10th, 11th, and 12th holes, he made more mistakes, allowing Danny Willett to put on the traditional green jacket given to the competition winner. But what happened to cause such a collapse?

To answer, it is relevant to analyze what Spieth said following his spectacular collapse:

"It was a dream on the go. I knew settling for par afterward would be enough to win. Maybe that's what sank me. I was not aggressive enough... I lacked concentration on my tee shots at the 11th and 12th holes... I did not take a deep enough breath before executing on the 12th hole. I rushed it."

In the case of Spieth, he already imagined himself the winner before starting the last part of the course. Looking into the future, he opted for a less aggressive approach than usual when choosing strategies. In addition, he became anxious about his performance and recognized deficiencies in his mental preparation at holes 11 and 12.

An athlete crumbles under pressure ("chokes") when their performance deteriorates dramatically under high stress. Instead of staying focused on their execution, they focus on the result and, therefore, realize the importance of what's at stake. They then change their state of mind, routine, and style of play, thus explaining the performance gap.

EXPERIENCING TUNNEL VISION

*****

> During tremendous pressure, the stress generated by an unprepared person causes the tunnel effect or tunnel vision. This is the brutal surge of adrenaline, which is at the origin of mental and physical failures, including visual disturbances.

Psycho-physiological reaction characterized by an adrenaline rush causes a loss of lucidity and a significant reduction in intellectual and physical performance. A narrowing field of vision can also accompany it. This narrowing is due to the foveal vision, which refers to the center of the field of vision, where visual acuity is at its highest, which works because of the eye's rapid movements (also called "saccades"). The fovea acts as a high-definition sensor over a very small part of our field of vision. The fovea is made up of cones. Under intense stress, our brain will instinctively accentuate this vision system and transmit a clear image, but reduced in size.

The hypnotic effect of brutal and sudden danger (mixed with anger, stress, and fear) during an intense moment of pressure causes tunnel vision. The gaze is blocked and focused on the source of the potential danger, making it impossible to see the rest of the environment.

Consequences of the Tunnel Effect

The tunnel effect prevents us from perceiving what's in our peripheral field of vision. It can also result in:

- significant acceleration of the pulse;

- elevated blood pressure;

- acceleration of respiratory rate;

- muscle contractions;

- uncontrolled breathing;

- hearing distortion;

- blocking of emotional control;

- uncontrolled or paralyzed movements.

If nature provides us with this instinctive metabolic reaction, it will survive in simpler environments. This tunnel effect is sometimes necessary during confrontation, such as when it's essential to concentrate on the precise materialization of the danger and to eliminate it at all costs as quickly as possible. But don't get stuck there longer than necessary.

Finding a peripheral vision that allows for reacting quickly to face a rapidly changing situation is necessary.

So, what should you do when experiencing tunnel vision?

Even if peripheral vision encompasses almost our entire field of vision and allows us to identify movements with excellent acuity, it is associated with a particular psychological state of calm.

The basic scientific principle is simple, but the implementation is more complicated.

The regulation of heart rhythm by the autonomic nervous system is influenced by breathing since inhalation temporarily inhibits the influence of the parasympathetic system and produces an accelerated heart rate. At the same time, exhalation stimulates the parasympathetic nervous system and produces a slowing heart. One of the objectives would be to regain control of your breathing as quickly as possible to lower your heart rate and blood pressure and to regain the most efficient peripheral vision possible.

The main objective is to open up one's field of vision, even if it means narrowing it again according to the necessary protection needs; stepping back to gain perspective is also a solution.

Learn to visualize the potential danger in all its forms without focusing on any particular detail. Develop a global vision of the situation and try to position yourself accordingly.

Given the multiplicity of external parameters during a competition, it's essential always to strive to:

- become aware of your environment;

- stay in control during the stress phase;

- not stay still (two steps back can change everything in terms of our lucidity and our perception of the environment);

- Do not remain inactive; decide: respond, defuse, fight or flee, whatever—but do something.

IMPACT ON PSYCHOMOTOR SKILLS

*****

> While you lose your lucidity, gestures, and movements can become awkward, slow, and less effective. Why? Because these movements, while in principle should be almost automatic, are anything but while you're losing lucidity. The movements feel new or foreign, without ease or fluidity.

The signs of stress in athletes are well known: the heart beats quickly, shortness of breath, muscles are tense, the legs tremble, and feelings of dizziness sometimes appear; the player is sweating, the mouth is dry, the stomach and intestines are sensitive; the technical gesture is disturbed because this gesture is "jerky," the player has lost fluidity, the "letting go"; and the more they concentrate on their technical gesture, the more it does not work. These are the adverse effects of stress hormones.

> Losing your technical gesture consists of involuntary contractions of the muscles of the forearms, hands, and legs that occur during a technical gesture requiring finesse and precision. It's more commonly called "the yips." Their origin is neurological and psychological, or even a mixture of the two. Specialists have named two main types: Those related to an acquired deterioration of motor function and those that appear to result from performance anxiety.

This pathology is most known in golf and is feared by its participants. Yips appear most often when putting. After ten or so years of playing, fifteen to twenty percent of players, especially competitive players, are affected.

While some continue their careers by adapting their technique, others are forced to capitulate. This happened to Ian Baker-Finch, winner of the British Open in 1991, and David Duval, the world's top-ranked player in 1999, both of whom became shadows of their former selves. Players report that the yips start with a loss of confidence that quickly turns to fear and blocking. The problem is at first periodic and only appears in specific situations. Then, the situation escalates.

Here's how golfer François Delamontagne described it:

"When I went up the club, the thousandth of a second between the end of the climb and the moment I started the descent, my brain would shut down. I no longer had control over my hands and completely let go of the club." The object could then fall 30 or 40 m behind him. "It was becoming dangerous for the spectators."

Faced with this spinning swing, Delamontagne began looking for solutions. He worked on his technique, trained more, and tried three mental trainers and a psychologist in a year and a half before surrendering. Mentally exhausted, he retires from the game at 35.

Although this type of story punctuates the history of golf, it is not unique to the sport.

Vice-world champion in the 2010 in the 50-meter rifle prone, Valérian Sauveplane, 34, had a bitter experience. Here again, the yips gradually set in. 2012, at the London Games, tremors intensified, and the automatisms decreased. Two years later, he experienced one of his worst crises at the world championships. This elite sniper could no longer aim. "I was no longer even able to align the end of the rifle with the target," Sauveplane said. "My front sight was blocked at the top. As soon as I saw the target, I pressed the trigger unwittingly. I got rid of the cartridge even though I was not centered. It was hell. I thought I was going crazy."

This phenomenon repeated the following year in the World Cup, where the yips took on a new form. Sauveplane could no longer put his hand on the rifle handle this time. "My hand was shaking like I was about to touch a snake. I had no finesse to put my finger on the trigger." But he would not give up, not like this. He looked for solutions to cure what he thought was a phobia. He changed his way of training, tried to take a step back and worry less about performance, and turned to psychotherapy. Then, he finally put a name to what he was experiencing. "The day I discovered these famous yips, I said, 'You're not crazy!' It doesn't solve the problem but is good for the mind."

The yips are not exclusive to golfers. It can even happen in tennis. The famous "crises in the service" of Guillermo Coria or Anna Kournikova, who committed 31 double faults in a single match during the 1999 Australian Open, are indeed yips, even if they weren't identified.

Many athletes unknowingly experience this, and some don't dare discuss it. There is indeed a feeling of helplessness.

No medication exists to treat yips, although treatments such as beta blockers have been tested without success. Athletes rely instead on technical work and muscle strengthening, all associated with mental preparation and cognitive-behavioral therapies.

Losing lucidity comes with several diverse effects. You need to identify how losing lucidity translates to you. Understanding what's happening to you under pressure is the first step to implementing a plan to improve your performance and well-being. This will enable you to enjoy your sport even more.

SECTION 2 WHAT CAUSES LOSS OF LUCIDITY?

THE IMPACT OF PRESSURE ON LUCIDITY

*****

Stage fright, fear, anxiety—athletes and competitors know them all. Fear of losing, fear of failure, fear of injury, fear of looking ridiculous in front of spectators or judges, fear of the opponent, and fear linked to actual physical danger—many have experienced some of these.

An emotion is an overall reaction to a specific situation. Fear, for example, is felt in the face of a perceived danger or threat. It can be manifested in caution, worry, anxiety, terror, horror, or panic and can even lead to the onset of a phobia. For an athlete approaching competition, fear is a normal response. It can be uncomfortable but is often a very normal part of competition, pushing them to take action when the time comes. It can be a stimulant that gives them strength and self-confidence.

Besides fear, emotions like anger, frustration, sadness, joy, shame, and disgust may arise throughout the competition, and with them, all the effects on the athlete and their behavior. Hence, they need to learn to identify, express, understand, and regulate emotions to manage them better and make them assets. Experience has shown that even if fear resumes in successive waves and overwhelms at different stages of the competition, it eventually passes. Therefore, The challenge can be to learn to use fear when it's present and to succeed in returning to normal as quickly as possible. However, fear can persist beyond validity if the athlete has emotional reactions they cannot manage or control.

Once, a participant told me before a karate tournament, "During training yesterday, everything was fine. But last night, I slept badly. This morning, my stomach was knotted. I started to think about the consequences of failure. I feel paralyzed by the stake. I can't seem to relax totally. What if I miss it? But why am I freaking out like this? Is it because I'm not at the top level? I blame myself for not having been consistent in training."

> In competition, the perception of a situation calls for global intelligence, which is perception through the senses, reasoning, emotions, experience, intuition, instant, and time. The athlete's perception of the situation and their conscience will determine their strategy for managing stress and emotions for a successful practice of their discipline.

Today, we talk a lot about stress—at work, with family, and in sports. Even children say they're stressed. Stress is an integral part of athletics. It can help mobilize the physical and mental energy necessary for optimal sports performance. However, it can also have harmful effects that reduce the athlete's performance potential.

In biology, stress corresponds to all the responses of an organism subject to pressures or constraints from its environment. According to the medical definition, it is a complex sequence of events provoking physiological and psychosomatic responses. These responses always depend on the individual's perception of their pressures. In everyday language, we speak of positive or negative stress depending on whether the induced effect is beneficial. We describe emotions similarly: Anger and sadness are negative emotions, while joy and love are positive.

Initially, a potential stimulus or stressor (a mild or severe event) causes a chain reaction and leads to responses. Between the two is what happens in the athlete's head: cognition, temperament, personal perception of the situation, knowledge, experience, and thoughts.

Whether in training or during competition, top athletes are confronted with multiple stimuli: environment (sports, family, friends, etc.), obligation to train, intensive preparation, management of their relationship with their coaches, aggressive competitors or teammates, emotional load, weight of responsibilities, media, travel, and distance from home, to name just several.

All top athletes know this pressure and the constraints of competition, but not necessarily with the same intensity. While some seem to approach things calmly and take a step back, others may feel intense physical discomfort and worries, which prevent them from reaching their highest level of performance.

Take the case of a hurdler. They must be in rhythm immediately, jumping over the hurdles without losing speed. They must not fall. Finally, their performance is aimed either at achieving personal goals such as a qualification or a victory or at the collective success of their team. That kind of pressure is recurrent among athletes.

The best athletes are, in principle, motivated, prepared, and have competition experience. They get along with their coach and teammates, regularly practice relaxation, and fully know their bodies. They're focused, have visualized the race, slept well, followed a healthy lifestyle, and are confident.

The athlete has already used all these resources at the right time to mobilize their energy and win. They will not doubt their ability to overcome the challenge, they will not think of failure, and they will not generate a negative response to the stress of the moment.

But sometimes, that same athlete does not feel in optimal shape. Perhaps they had a dispute with their coach or a personal concern. Physiological and psychosomatic responses that do not conform to the moment's needs might be generated. Resistance or adaptability to the situation are likely to be altered.

While things sometimes naturally return to order, a feeling of discomfort in which the athlete is drawn into a spiral of negative thoughts and mental ruminations may also emerge. Very quickly, they can blame themselves or feel guilty, becoming aggressive or anxious. The coach or the entourage may repeat: "Go, relax," "Have confidence," "Let go," "Concentrate," "Do not be stressed," or "Focus on the fundamentals." Still, these exaltations will be useless if the athletes don't have specific tools to adapt to this situation.

The stress level, the intensity of the emotions, and the response depend on the person's perception. An athlete knows what's likely to provoke unpleasant emotions that may harm their performance, but they can change their way of seeing things if they want to.

Practiced regularly—before, during, and after competitions—relaxation makes it possible to feel more at ease physically and mentally. Once tensions are removed, the cleared mind can work more efficiently, intuitively, and simply. Mindfulness meditative practices help you understand your feelings and perception of events. You'll be able to observe your relationship with emotions and free yourself from their grip when they affect your performance.

THE INTENSE DESIRE TO ATTAIN SOMETHING

*****

Desiring a particular result or achievement too intensely causes excessive arousal and interferes with memory decision-making. When the desire is too intense, it is characterized by the reshaping of the neural pathways to create a process of desire, habit, pleasure, and emotional regulation. The loss of lucidity comes from only thinking about the outcome, no longer being aware of what's happening in the game, and being completely disconnected from real-time. Dopamine is the addiction hormone; it powers the reward circuit and is stimulated by the pleasure of winning.

Dopamine—aka "the pleasure molecule"—is one of the many chemicals that serve as a neurotransmitter in the brain. Like norepinephrine, dopamine is synthesized from the amino acid tyrosine. Dopamine involves motor control, attention, pleasure, motivation, sleep, memory, and cognition. It also plays a role in behavior.

Dopamine is the primary neurotransmitter involved in the reward circuit in the brain, but other molecules are also involved: GABA, norepinephrine, and serotonin. Drug addiction is linked to a disruption of the reward circuit because drugs like cocaine, morphine, and heroin stimulate the release of dopamine. Drugs produce a feeling of satisfaction that leads to dependence among addicts.

If you become obsessed with goals and results, you can lose lucidity, so you must be aware of your goals and behaviors. Never become consumed by results. Keep focus on the process and build momentum to achieve your goals.

BEING IMPATIENT

*****

If you know that you always tend to rush and not analyze your opponent, you will quickly realize that your way of doing things does not necessarily suit all foes.

Let's use sparring as an example. You must take the time to analyze either in advance by video or, if none exists, at the time of combat. If you always do the same thing instead of taking the time to analyze and curtail your technique to your opponent, you won't be very successful.

I made this mistake recently. Why? Because I was impulsive, impatient, and feared missing the right opportunity. It's often the lack of patience that will make you repeat mistakes. Rushing and letting your emotions take over have much in common. Both will result in a loss of lucidity and your capacity for analysis.

MAKING A MISTAKE

*****

It's been said that football is a sport of mistakes, and I think the same can be said of tennis. Which player will first hit the ball out of bounds or directly into the net? After all, tennis is relatively simple: Putting one more ball in play than the opponent.

That being said, if you're a tennis player, you will miss shots—a lot!

Making mistakes is part of the tennis player's reality, but they can become very frustrating when accumulated. The game can be mentally challenging.

There are always ups and downs in a tennis game. A player may win or lose two or three points consecutively. Making repeated mistakes can cause you to lose lucidity as your attention drifts inward, causing your inner voice to become louder and more distracting.

Making mistakes over and over can lead to frustration, tension, and loss of lucidity. When you feel like you're constantly making the same mistakes and facing challenges or continually making efforts that are never rewarded, you're likely to feel frustrated. And when you feel frustrated, it often means that the results should be different.

How do you keep calm and maintain clarity during the mental storm of playing poorly and making mistakes?

Then, once you've done that, how do you beat the frustration in tennis?

Let's say you play 50 to 100 matches in a season; you'll probably only play three to five well. For the rest, you have to do with what's working best that day. Those are the implicit rules of the game. If you don't accept them, you won't be able to go as far as you want.

The message of frustration is an interesting signal: Your brain thinks you could do better. This can be a good thing because it may cause you to strive to improve. It means a solution is within your reach, and you must approach things differently. It signals that you must be more flexible and learn to let go.

When you feel frustration, it's usually caused by focusing your attention and inner language on what's already gone wrong.

Are you in confidence or doubt? In gratitude or frustration? If you focus on what hasn't worked, you'll likely repeat those mistakes.

Successful top-level entrepreneurs and athletes will oscillate between focusing on the present—to be fully immersed in the moment—and on the future—to plan their agenda or training schedule or anticipate any difficulties that might arise in a negotiation or during a tennis match, for example.

Successful people don't wait for success; they constantly prepare for it. Paying attention to what you cannot control inevitably leads to helplessness, which is the root of all emotions unsuited to performance, such as frustration, loss of motivation, and anger.

So, to free yourself from this helplessness, you must learn to focus only on what you can control.

Here is the testimony of an amateur golfer:

"A few months ago, for the first time in my life, I threw a club after yet another failed shot during a bad period. And I opened Pandora's box. Since, I have thrown clubs at least six times, planted my 9-iron in a slightly soft fairway—but I filled the hole, threw two or three balls in the rough after grazing putts, and kicked my bag. And the tolerance threshold for a miss before explosion is increasingly low.

I cannot stand putts that graze, and it happens to me a lot despite spending four hours per week putting. I'm less tolerant of missed shots and get annoyed with each one. I can't stand it anymore, so yes, my expectations are too high. That is not the question.

How do you manage anger and avoid exploding? Of course, it eats energy.

I've always been quite angry, especially when things don't go as they should."

Tiger Woods developed a good approach: you draw an imaginary line five or ten meters after the stroke to be played. Before the line, we have the right to be frustrated and rehash the missed shot, but as soon as we pass it, we must be on to the next move. So, we miss a shot, we allow ourselves a little 'damn it,' and then we cross the line, and it's over. If you feel the anger still exists, take a deep breath and say, 'I am golfing, something I love. I am grateful for that; a bad start does not prevent the par.' And you cross the line in the right direction, calm and lucid!

Of course, it's easier said than done, especially the first few times, especially when you play badly, but it comes quickly if you practice it in training.

EMOTIONS RISING FROM LOSING

*****

Having a good mindset isn't winning when everything is going well. It's not being calm when things are going well. It's staying the course even when nothing's going your way.

Let's say you're playing tennis with a friend who's less experienced than you. You're expecting to win easily, but today, your friend is playing much better, maybe getting a little lucky, and the match is close. You sense that you're getting frustrated and not even having fun. It's becoming all about winning. Your state of mind has changed. You're aggressive, you become impatient, and you're starting to make mistakes you rarely make. This enhances your frustration and causes you to lose your lucidity. You don't have a clear mind, and it seems you cannot return to calmness and focus.

It's time to clear your mind, take a deep breath, and focus on the present moment.

INJURIES AND SICKNESS

*****

While practicing sports that involve the perfection of body formation, such as gymnastics, diving, tumbling, or figure skating, the athlete will fall and possibly be injured. Each of these events is encoded and stored in the individual's memory. At one point, the athlete's ability to cope with all these memories is endangered by a triggering event. It may be one fall, one injury, or the pressure generated by an upcoming competition. This triggering event can generate fear, a blockage that will persist forever, even permanently, causing the inability to perform a particular movement. There is a blockage related to the functioning of the nervous system.

> Triggered by memories of injuries and accidents, the nervous system interprets the fall or new injury as a threat. To protect the athlete, it issues a response that results in paralysis.

LOSS OF LUCIDITY ASSOCIATED WITH AN UNBALANCED DIET

*****

> Your diet impacts your lucidity. An optimal supply of nutrients will ensure good brain performance throughout the day. Foods that are good for memory and focus are nutrient-rich foods low in low-density lipoproteins (bad cholesterol) and sugars. Carbohydrates must be distributed throughout the day for a constant energy level.

Full breakfast

Studies show that eating a full breakfast improves performance and reduces memory and concentration problems before noon. These effects are more pronounced if the breakfast is rich in good carbohydrates, like oats and bananas. In fact, after breakfast, an optimal glucose level promotes intellectual performance. Skipping breakfast is associated with fatigue. To reach and keep the desired blood-glucose level, it is recommended to favor foods that naturally contain carbohydrates and are rich in fiber but to reduce those high in added sugars. Eating a little protein at breakfast and reducing fatty or non-nutritious foods is also essential.

Omega 3

Most of our brain is made up of fat. Myelin, the sheath surrounding nerve cells called neurons, contains 70 percent lipids. This sheath promotes the creation of new connections (synapses) between them. That's why we associate good fats with a healthy brain. Indeed, more and more studies establish a link between high consumption of vegetable fats (olive oil, seeds, or nuts) and marine omega-3 and reduced cognitive decline in the elderly. A diet low in omega-3 could weaken the structure and composition of the membranes of neurons, thereby affecting brain chemistry. In addition, a diet too rich in saturated fat—mostly from animal sources—and trans-fat can degenerate neurons and reduce intellectual performance.

Some sources of fat that are good for memory and concentration are salmon, sardines, tuna, olive oil, pumpkin, flax seeds, chia seeds, and avocado.

EFFECT OF DEHYDRATION ON BRAIN FUNCTIONS

*****

> The first signs of dehydration are a decrease in alertness and concentration.

People with mild dehydration may also experience fatigue and headaches. It seems that most of us experience these effects regularly. As dehydration continues, the blood volume decreases, making the blood thicker and increasing the heart rate. This hinders the body's ability to dissipate heat, which is why symptoms of sunstroke can appear so quickly. When the body is overheated and lacks water, physical exercise becomes more complex, you lose your lucidity, and you can even feel emotionally fragile.

Effect of dehydration on sports performance

We know we're supposed to drink plenty of water. But did you know that hydration is a crucial factor in performance and injury prevention in athletes?

Your body is about 60 percent water, two-thirds of which is in your cells. This rate varies according to age, weight, sex, and muscular mass.

Water is essential for your survival: If your body loses more than 15 percent of its weight in water, death can occur, so you can only survive three to five days without drinking. Sure, water hydrates, but it also eliminates waste and transports nutrients, among other things.

Among the most hydrated tissues and organs are the brain (75 percent), the lungs (79 percent), the kidneys (83 percent), the blood

(83 percent), the heart (79 percent), and the muscles (73 percent). These organs are susceptible to dehydration. For example, the cerebrospinal fluid, which protects your brain, is composed almost exclusively of water (99 percent). It's pretty easy to see how important water is to your health.

Daily water intake and losses

Besides drinking water, you get some from food and lose it through natural processes.

On average, you lose 2.6 liters of water per day through urine (1.5 liters), stool (100 milliliters), perspiration (300 milliliters), pulmonary expiration (500 milliliters) and sweating (0.5 liters, although professional athletes may lose up to 10 liters). This is why it's important to hydrate regularly throughout the day to compensate for these losses, especially if you're active. Water loss varies significantly with the type of physical activity, temperature, and humidity. But don't wait: arrive at training or competition already well-hydrated!

Remember that you can never make up 100 percent of water lost during physical exercise, so starting your training or competition already hydrated is essential. The most effective method is to follow a daily water plan and check the color of your urine in the morning on an empty stomach—the clearer it is, the better hydrated you are.

A minimum water plan:

• After waking up: one to two glasses of water

• Breakfast: one hot drink such as coffee, tea, herbal tea, or an infusion.

• In the morning, a half-liter of water

• At noon: at least three glasses of water

• In the afternoon, a half-liter of water

• Dinner: three or four glasses of water

Trying to catch up on dehydration at the last moment does not work, so don't bother chugging a liter of water a few minutes before your training session. In addition to not hydrating yourself effectively, you'll feel heavy and bloated.

If you are practicing in a sport with weight categories, not drinking before weighing in to lose your last pounds is not a good solution. Arriving dehydrated at a competition already impacts your performance and increases the risk of injuries. In combat sports, the consequences of a blow to the head or strangulation can be made worse if the brain is poorly hydrated.

How should you hydrate during training?

One percent water loss can equate to a 10 percent decrease in performance. When water loss is four percent, the drop in performance can vary between 40 and 60 percent depending on the surrounding temperature. And the warmer it is, the more the performance deteriorates.

This represents only 480 milliliters of water for a 75-kilogram man and 320 milliliters for a 60-kilogram woman.

To avoid this, drink 150 to 200 milliliters of water every 20 minutes, although this should be tested individually depending on your gastric tolerance. You should especially drink before you're thirsty because the feeling of thirst is a late signal of dehydration during exercise. If you are suddenly thirsty, it is because your cells have been dehydrated for a long time.

The cell rehydration process is very long. Your intestines absorb the water you drink, which travels through your digestive system and enters your vascular system, interstitial fluid, and finally, your cells.

Generally, tap water is enough for short physical activities (60 to 90 minutes) and at temperatures above 68 degrees Fahrenheit. If you don't love the taste of water, you can add flavoring, but be careful not to add too many carbohydrates or sugar, such as syrup or honey. Too much can slow your stomach's emptying time and slow hydration and water's effectiveness.

Use clothing adapted to your sport.

Also, think about your clothes. Cotton, for example, prevents perspiration from evaporating, and your body takes longer to cool down. There's a reason technical clothing lets perspiration through.

For practitioners of judo, jiu jitsu, or any other sport where a gi is worn, remember to open or even take off your jacket regularly so your perspiration can evaporate.

And after training?

Post-session water consumption is just as important for rehydration and recovery. Even slight dehydration can significantly impact muscle recovery—muscles are around 73 percent water, don't forget! Drink one to 1.5 liters of water after your session, but not too quickly.

It is also recommended that the waters be varied. Try Perrier, for example, which is very popular among athletes. The bubbly beverage has bicarbonates, a little sodium, and some magnesium and can be a pleasant change from flat water.

In addition, dehydration can affect the athlete's health, causing impairment of intellectual capacity, dizziness, muscle and tendon disorders (breakdowns, elongations, contractures), digestive disorders, cardiac disorders, and heat stroke during exercise.

| Dehydration causes immediate damage to our mental capacities. |

According to a study by Harvard Medical School, it has recently been found to cause shrinkage of brain tissue and a corresponding increase in ventricular volume. Like the leaves of waterless plants, brain cells appear to dry out and contract.

The brain is up to 85 percent water, which allows it to function well. Several studies have shown moderate dehydration decreases alertness while increasing fatigue and anxiety. Concentration and short-term memory can also be impaired, so a clinical relationship undoubtedly exists between dehydration and cognitive mechanisms.

New research shows that dehydration, even after physical exercise, disrupts cognitive skills and changes the activity of some brain regions. But the good news is that rehydrating restores regular brain activity.

Do you suffer from problems with concentration, mood, memory, or coordination?

Maybe it's because your brain lacks water. Dehydration, even slight, sometimes affects cognitive function. How? The Georgia Institute of Technology in Atlanta, known as Georgia Tech, provides new answers.

Neurons and other cells in our brain are primarily made up of water and cannot function without it. Several scientific studies have looked at the effect of lack of water on the shape and functions of different brain structures. Some have found variations in volume; others have not. Cognitive impairment is described in some instances, while nothing like it is observed in others.

To get to the bottom of it, Matthew Wittbrodt and his colleagues at Georgia Tech recruited 13 healthy volunteers with an average age of 24. They exercised them on a treadmill for two-and-a-half hours, alternating 45 minutes of walking with 15-minute breaks. This was enough to cause a water loss of about three percent.

In the first session, the volunteers drank as much water as they lost but did not hydrate at all in the second. Then, they were asked to perform a simple and repetitive visuospatial task, such as pressing a button with the right index finger when they saw specific shapes appear on a screen. At the same time, the structure and activity of their brains were measured by magnetic resonance imaging (MRI).

As a result, when volunteers drink water while exercising, their cerebral ventricles (the fluid-filled cavities in the center of the brain that allow them to flush toxins) contract. Conversely, the ventricles swell in those who do not hydrate, as if to compensate for the lack of water in the brain, while the surrounding brain structures shrink. This happens to the thalamus, a cerebral hub integrating sensory data, and the cerebellum, which helps coordination and movement. In addition, after exercise, dehydrated participants saw their performance in the visuomotor task drop by 16 percent, compared to only 8 percent for volunteers who drank.

> Dehydration can impair a person's ability to think clearly.

Researchers found that athletes who lost fluid equal to two percent of their weight took a hit to their cognition. Even this mild-to-moderate level of dehydration led to attention problems and impaired decision-making. In particular, dehydration led to impaired tasks requiring attention, motor coordination, and executive function, including map recognition, grammatical reasoning, mental math, and proofreading.

Researchers concluded that these brain changes and the variations in osmolarity (differences in pressure on either side of cells) that result from lack of water affect brain activity and cognitive skills.

BRAIN FREEZE: EFFECT OF COLD TEMPERATURE

*****

Cold is a relative sensation, and everyone perceives it differently. But if the feeling of cold is too much, your body will go into a "safety mode." If this happens, you're in a difficult situation.

Concretely, in a hydrothermal shock, your brain will initiate its emergency procedure to protect you. First, we will significantly increase our energy consumption to burn as many calories as possible. We draw on the stored reserves, which will burn very quickly.

Then, if that's not enough, part of the blood that must supply our muscles with oxygen will be redirected to the heart and vital organs to provide them with maximum heat. Our heart will also start to beat much faster to speed up blood flow and organ warming, making us breathless so that we cannot put our heads underwater.

So, we have to acclimate because it keeps us from panicking in the middle of the water.

PHYSICAL FATIGUE AND EXHAUSTION

*****

Sleep is essential to proper brain functioning, and lack of sleep leads to a sharp decline in cognitive abilities, such as verbal skills, concentration problems, or difficulty solving problems.

Adults generally need seven to nine hours of sleep to maintain optimal cognitive performance. Some people will notice problems with concentration and memory that can go as far as mental confusion; the speed at which brain information is transmitted seems slower, and focusing on something becomes very difficult. It may happen that short-term memory does not hold everything. Cognitive symptoms are challenging to live with because they make work even more complicated, increase fatigue and stress, and can cause a feeling of isolation.

A lack of sleep decreases attention span. Without getting enough sleep, we cannot pay as much attention to our senses as we would like. Therefore, fatigue results in that strange feeling of distraction.

SECTION 3 ENTERING THE LUCIDITY STATE.

INTENTION IS THE KEY THAT TURNS MINDSET INTO ACTION.

*****

Now that you understand what causes loss of lucidity, we need to explore what makes you enter the lucid state. Lucidity is impossible without activation and stimulation, which can occur through intention or being thrust into a threatening situation.

Why is intention so powerful?

> Intention directs attention. The quantum physics of the law of attraction shows that it develops as soon as you focus on something. As soon as you turn your attention to your training in swimming, it is developing. If you pay attention to your skills, they develop. The intention is ultimately the joystick that allows you to direct your attention and enter the lucid state.

Having goals, visualizing them, making affirmations, and turning them into intentions all focus your mind on what you want and increase your chances of manifesting it in your life.

An intention is more than just a goal to achieve. Behind each of your actions hides an intention. Depending on the person who acts, there are a multitude of intentions for the same action. Here's an example:

Michelle and Julia must perform the same action: swim to the other end of a body of water at 10 degrees Celsius. Depending on their intention, their actions will be experienced differently. If Michelle intends to swim this length in this cold water "because you have to," she will swim without real focus and be unable to use this training optimally for the upcoming competition. If Julia "wishes to put all her efforts into this training for the upcoming competition," she will have the optimal concentration to reap the maximum benefits and put her body and soul into it. She will most likely be able to induce a lucid state.

When you don't give yourself a precise intention, your mind is in automatic mode, and you deprive yourself of an essential asset in your preparation.

Emitting an intention is consciously choosing a direction for your day, week, cycle, and life.

Emitting intentions allows you to:

• Become aware of what motivates your actions;

• Give meaning to them;

• Be more focused on your action, to be in the here and now;

• Learn to differentiate actions that serve your intentions from those that do not serve them;

• Be focused on your life goals and put in place quality actions to achieve them;

• Be the creator of your existence and manifest what you want.

An intention begins with a goal. Your imagination is your only limit. But to discover the purpose, you must go through two crucial stages: visualization and affirmation.

So, a goal means formulating what you want.

Example: "I want to qualify for the New York City Marathon."

Visualization: Make yourself comfortable, as if to meditate, and close your eyes. You will now visualize your goal as if you were making it come true. Use your imagination. Concentrate on your feelings. Do you feel joy, gratitude, relief, pride? Feel it in your body.

Example: Imagine picking up your welcome pack from the New York registration center and feeling excited and proud!

Affirmation: Turn that feeling into an affirmation that goes with your goal.

Example: "I am excited to run the New York City Marathon."

Intention: Now transform this goal into intentions by defining your actions to achieve it.

Example: "I will check the requirements to qualify for the New York City Marathon."

WITH INTENTION COMES MOTIVATION

*****

> Both intention and motivation are essential in reaching a lucid state. Intention gives direction; motivation gives intensity and persistence.

Motivation prompts an individual to act in a given direction with intensity and pushes them to maintain their actions. It's commonly accepted that motivation is a key performance factor. Just keep in mind that motivation without intention will not drive you where you want to go since, without intention, you have no direction.

Every day, we do activities for pleasure, while we do other less-pleasant things because we have to or because we force ourselves to.

We practice sports to learn a physical activity that offers new knowledge, to better ourselves, and to achieve new goals. One example is the exhilarating sensations of speed experienced by athletes in many disciplines.

Tips for working on your intentions and motivation:

#1: You can't get what you want until you know what it is. Expressing your intentions allows you to find out through practice, day after day.

#2: Focus your energy on what you want, not what you don't want. Thinking is creative, so it might become real if you focus on what you don't want to happen. Always write down your wishes, affirmations, and intentions in the first person and the present tense as if you were already there.

#3: Only want what you really think is possible. For example, there is no point in wasting energy wishing to win the Tour de France rather than focusing on giving your best effort in a regional race and trying to finish in the top 10.

You must honestly believe in your goal and your ability to make it happen.

#4: Cut out your limiting beliefs, which will not allow your goal to become reality. If you want to participate in your first triathlon when you believe you can never overcome your fear of open water, that will never happen.

#5: Have a clear intention. The clearer the intention, the more precise the answer.

#6: Be detached. The more you are detached from the result, the more it will be accelerated. Don't worry about winning.

#7: Have gratitude for the life you have. The future is created in the present. In the present, you will determine who you want to become. So, it's essential to have a genuine desire that drives you. Because if it drives you, your body's biochemistry will change, your posture will change, and your thoughts will change—and all of this together means your future will change. So, an intention is not just a thought; it is also a posture and a way of being.

#8: Be centered. Being centered means that you are neither extraordinarily negative nor highly positive. If a task is done, good; if it's not done, fine; you'll do it soon. The more you're detached from the results, the more focused you'll be.

LEVELS OF CONSCIOUSNESS

*****

Subconscious and conscious are the two levels of an individual's consciousness, to which some add the superconscious, which corresponds to the spiritual state of awakening.

What is the conscious?

Our five senses govern consciousness: sight, hearing, touch, taste, and smell, as well as reflection and the capacity for analysis.

Consciousness is limited, as it performs between five and seven tasks simultaneously. For example, concentrate on a news channel while reading the ticker at the bottom of the screen, write an email, and be on the phone with a friend. It's feasible but not very easy.

What is the subconscious?

The subconscious represents all that is not conscious. It is the reservoir of our innate automatisms.

Our subconscious protects us and can handle thousands of bits of information simultaneously.

The subconscious contains the thoughts and actions of the individual. It is the reservoir of automation:

Body: walking, physical reaction to a stimulus, instinctive impulses;

Mind: speaking, dreams, verbal impulses.

Our internal hard drive has unlimited storage capacity for records, at least since birth, intuition, memories, fears, phobias, traumas, and many other things.

The subconscious is a part of consciousness that has transformed into something that is no longer treatable by consciousness. These are automatisms and artificial reflexes.

The subconscious comes into play by connecting your intentions and goals to the Reticular Activating System (RAS). The RAS is a reticular formation component found in the anterior-most segment of the brainstem. The reticular formation receives input from the spinal cord, sensory pathways, thalamus, and cortex and has efferent connections throughout the nervous system. By helping you focus on what is important to you, the RAS acts as a filter between your conscious mind and your subconscious. The RAS takes instructions from your conscious mind and transmits to your subconscious mind what is relevant for you to notice and what to focus on to achieve your goals.

The subconscious does not need to be burdened with too much information; it needs to know your intention and what's important to you. The RAS acts like a radar or an unconscious filter by performing this relevant sorting. The RAS identifies what does or does not deserve your attention among the many signals received. And as soon as the RAS considers information vital to you, it activates your perceptual processes to absorb it. The RAS is a valuable ally that only lets through helpful information for achieving what matters to you.

The RAS is working to get you what you are looking for or fleeing from. If you intend to escape a problematic situation, your RAS will activate to notice anything contributing to the problem's presence. And if you want to seize the opportunities of a situation, your RAS will activate to allow you to see, hear, and feel all that contributes to encountering opportunities.

The RAS is at the service of your intentions. But the RAS has no opinion on the content of your intention. It can serve the best of you or the worst. It is essential to know how to give relevant instructions to your subconscious to optimize its configuration. Your subconscious just needs a clear representation of what you want. Your subconscious will stay awake and alert you to anything that can help you achieve your goals. The RAS doesn't distinguish between the real and the imaginary. You match your subconscious with your conscious will to achieve something by setting your intention.

Establishing your intention is one way of preparing your subconscious mind and your RAS for the path to your goal.

Establishing your intention is a powerful way to direct your conscious energy and attention to your future goal. This keeps your subconscious and your RAS focused on the desired outcome.

By defining our intention for the desired result and the path to achieve it, we influence our inner and outer reality, setting a new chain of events directly connected to our subconscious. By setting your intention, you send a positive message to your RAS to direct your attention to what you want.

LUCIDITY THROUGH THE ACTION OF THE RAS

*****

> Activation was introduced to account for the observation that the organism does not always function with the same intensity. Through phases of total sleep, diffuse wakefulness, passivity, intense interest, and excitement, activation represents behavior's intensive, energetic dimension. Early on, researchers were interested in its influence on the efficiency of perceptual, cognitive, or motor processes. Activation is arousal and awareness of the environment and self, which is achieved through the action of the RAS on the brain stem and cerebral cortex.

The RAS comprises four main components, each containing groupings of nuclei: the locus coeruleus, raphe nuclei, posterior tuberomammillary hypothalamus, and pedunculopontine tegmentum.

Each is unique in the neuropeptides they release:

•   The locus coeruleus is activated directly by orexin from the lateral hypothalamus and releases norepinephrine in response. It functions primarily upon waking and in arousal.

•   The raphe nuclei are serotonergic. They play a role in various bodily functions, including pain sensation, mood regulation, and circadian rhythms, and contribute to arousal and attention.

•   The tuberomammillary nucleus is histaminergic and is the brain's primary source of histamine projections. It is essential in wakefulness and cognition, projecting to the forebrain, which plays a vital role in arousal.

• The lateral and dorsal pedunculopontine tegmentum contains primarily cholinergic neurons. Cholinergic neurons promote desynchronization of the brain, allowing the body to switch from slow sleep rhythms to high-frequency, low-amplitude wake rhythms.

The lateral hypothalamus largely activates these centers, which releases the neuropeptide orexin in response to light hitting the eyes. This neuropeptide stimulates arousal and the transition from sleep to wakefulness. The groupings of neurons that make up the RAS are ultimately responsible for attention, arousal, modulation of muscle tone, ability to focus, and lucidity state.

The level of activation is affected by many factors. Some examples are stressors such as physical exertion, air temperature, drugs such as caffeine, and emotions such as fear, anxiety, love, surprise, or just interest.

LACTIC ACID, FATIGUE, AND THE MIND-BODY CONNECTION

*****

How can you begin the activation process necessary for entering the lucid state when you feel tired? Fighting fatigue is never easy. Heavy legs, contracted forearms, the urge to vomit—some training regimens require an extremely high resistance capacity.

You have no doubt experienced the feeling of nauseous fatigue during intense exertion. This can happen more easily when you're not warmed up enough. This unpleasant sensation is linked to the specific functioning of an energy-production chain allowing muscle contraction called anaerobic glycolysis, more commonly known as the lactic chain.

After a few seconds of intense exertion, the muscle's explosive energy reserves are depleted, and you must start using the sugars stored in the muscle, liver, and blood to prolong the effort. The problem is that this technique for producing muscle contractions is accompanied by annoying side effects, such as reduced coordination and gestural precision, difficulty producing contractions, loss of lucidity, or even the urge to vomit. These effects will last until the athlete stops exercising or decreases its intensity to change the type of energy they are using, switching to a predominantly aerobic energy supply.

The challenge for many sports is producing movements of constant quality and efficiency with relatively short periods and complete lucidity.

It is crucial for maintaining gestural precision, coordination, and lucidity to:

• Unleash near-maximum power, if necessary, very quickly in the event/competition;

• Improve your ability to recover from these specific efforts, in particular with the oxygenation of the body;

• Improve your physical and mental tolerance of this type of effort.

The rules of practical lactic-acid work are simple:

• Long and passive recovery (four to six minutes in the examples);

• Short and very intense series (less than three intermittent minutes);

• The intensity is close to maximum, relaunched several times during the series by splitting the effort.

Here are some workout examples to build your capacity for resistance and to maintain a lucidity state even during an intense effort:

Circuit 1: 3 x 15

Resistance can be expressed in many ways depending on the sport. As soon as you exceed fifteen seconds of effort, you must be able to continue developing high levels of muscle power. For intermittent efforts, this first phase of endurance is expressed at full power for up to one minute. This circuit will seek to improve the first minute of intense effort.

- 15 seconds of push-ups; do as many as possible in the allotted time

- 15 seconds of sprinting in place; do as many steps as possible

- 15 seconds of tuck jumps; do as many jumps as possible

- 2 burpees

After a cardiovascular warm-up specific to your sport, do four to six sets, taking four minutes of recovery between each set.

Circuit 2: the longest 90 seconds

In some sports, another form of resistance occurs between 90 and 120 seconds, repeating intense actions and fighting against the drop in intensity. A great exercise is to establish a simple circuit, which we will try to repeat as many times as possible during a given time.

- 10 kettlebell swings

- Quadrupedal movement (four meters)

- Four frog jumps

- Quadrupedal movement (four meters)

- 10 mountain climbers

- Repeat, but begin with mountain climbers and end with kettlebell swings

After warm-up, do four to six sets, taking four minutes of recovery between each set.

Circuit 3: the stop-and-go circuit

Lastly, lactic endurance is expressed in the ability to boost intensity after a phase of extreme fatigue. This is where longer circuits with sporadic maximum effort will pay off. Here is an example of a circuit without rest between workouts. Each exercise should be performed at maximum intensity.

- Shuffle in a square for 30 seconds

- 10 sprints in place (each leg should tap the floor five times) and two repeated group jumps for 15 seconds

- 10 burpees

- 10 push-ups

After the warm-up, do four sets, taking four minutes of recovery between each set.

Circuit 4: the infernal shuttle

Finally, it is crucial to recover correctly between efforts and to be able to continue. This quality of recovery is mainly linked to an athlete's ability to use oxygen. This time, the intensity of the circuits should be slightly lower and the recovery a little shorter to prevent the athlete from fully recovering. We suggest the following session: In front of a partner positioned at the other end of the room, shuttle between them and your starting position. When you work, the partner rests, and vice versa. This involves completing eight sets of 30 seconds of effort and 30 seconds of rest at a distance of about 15 meters.

- Six short shuffles left and right;

- Sprint to your partner at the other end of the room;

- Six burpees, clapping the partner's hand at each repetition;

- Sprint back to the starting point;

- Repeat until the end of 30 seconds, and switch roles afterward.

It is essential to maintain the same number of repetitions for each set.

AWARENESS

*****

There is no lucidity without awareness. Awareness includes your environment and inner dialogue. To enter the lucidity state, you need to slow down your thoughts.

The body is one of the foundations of self-awareness. Although it constantly transmits much information to the brain, we are far from knowing it fully. It's even possible to perceive our body surprisingly if our sensory information or beliefs are modified during visualization or hypnosis sessions, for example.

Self-awareness is apprehending external phenomena (e.g., sensations via the sensory organs) and/or interior (e.g., our emotional and postural states). Awareness of oneself is a process of reflecting on one's experience and relationship with the outside world and others. It is an interaction between thoughts, sensations, and emotions. In sports, the athlete simultaneously plays their body and mind. Their body-mind symbiosis allows them to produce a physical performance that will be measured and judged. It appears logical that the professional athlete develops an expertise in the relationship to their body and their psycho-affective processes and that they can have a high self-awareness of their body by movement.

Self-awareness is about developing the ability to listen to signals emitted by the body and the mind (internal dialogue) in their interactions with the external environment.

Some benefits to self-awareness:

• it allows athletes to develop autonomy by offering them better knowledge of themselves, which also increases their degree of responsibility;

• athletes will also become better at self-observation and correcting themselves;

• people can focus their attention on the external environment and offer appropriate responses (thus improving lucidity in action);

• increased ability to recognize a state of fatigue that could lead to the injury.

Self-awareness develops early and is integral to motor learning delivered by parents and educators.

How can you develop awareness?

• Question yourself about your impressions, feelings, and internal comments about the progress and the quality of the realization of a gestural sequence—where in your body? How do you know it? How does it feel? —before giving its technical point of view or its general appreciation ("it's good" or "it's bad").

• Ask yourself regularly how you feel before, during, and after training; on what and where are your thoughts and attention centered? What did you learn from your competition, session, and exercise?

• Name your internal states something other than "stress" (e.g., worried, tense, in doubt, excited, impatient, feverish, fear of losing, fear of winning, moved, etc.).

• Put yourself in the coach's position: "If I were your coach, what advice would I give?"

•   Introduce elements and/or specific work sessions of meditation, breathing, mental imagery, relaxation, or yoga during warmups, physical preparation sessions, or the return to calm.

Self-awareness requires more patience, but it allows us to focus on reality. It makes us aware of what we can and cannot do and helps us understand what we can learn. It generally keeps us from chasing chimeras and not knowing our limits. It makes us focus our energy wisely.

Self-awareness can allow you to update limiting beliefs about yourself and others and act accordingly. However, gaining complete self-awareness is impossible, leaving a critical field for a coach's external gaze and analysis. This is because self-awareness is, in reality, a misunderstanding of self since it is a fundamentally subjective process; many mechanisms, such as self-esteem, bad faith, and unconsciousness, obscure our perception of ourselves.

PROPRIOCEPTION, WHAT IS IT?

*****

We all know our five senses: hearing, smell, touch, vision, and taste. But there's another one that we use constantly: proprioception. But what is it, and what are its roles?

Proprioception is the knowledge, conscious or not, of the position of the different parts of our body in space. More scientifically, it is the nerve information sent to the brain from the muscles, tendons, joints, and tissues. Comparable to a sixth sense about the environment outside the body, this technique, regularly used by physiotherapists, can treat injuries often related to joints.

From the Latin propitious and reception, the word proprioception means "own conscience" or "deep sensitivity."

Proprioception development

Proprioception relies on the brain's plasticity, ability to reorganize its neural circuits according to its resources, and the tasks it has to perform. Motor learning constantly creates neural connections, and our actions change our brains. This is why it takes many repetitions to strengthen the connections, and this is why proprioception plays a significant role, through movement, in the development of the body representation, which is built very gradually during childhood.

The fetus is in flexion in the uterus, which allows it to test its proprioception during sharp movements of extension and coiling. The brain slowly begins to take control of these movements.

Later, small children develop their proprioceptive system by moving, which they should be encouraged to do. They gradually recognize the different parts of their body and the bodies of others, and at around 3 years old, they can roughly draw a human. The body representation is not completed until around 11-12 years old. Thereafter, it is constantly updated according to our actions and what we are undergoing, such as a change in weight, a growth spurt in adolescence, or an injury.

Developing proprioception can take you to new heights, like professional dancers or when a musician plays without looking at their fingers.

When they hear the word proprioception, many think of work on unstable surfaces or trampolines that we do at the physiotherapist after an injury. Proprioception is also found in the weight room, on the field, at the professional level, and in large clubs. But standing on an unstable plateau, a Bosu ball, for example, is not proprioception. It is more of a work of balance, which can be enjoyable but also has limits.

Proprioception allows us to control our limbs without looking directly at them. And without it, the life we know would be impossible.

So, it is at the origin of coordination and skill. These two qualities form the basis of motor skills. Good proprioception is essential for maintaining posture and coordinating movements.

Spatial localization

Beyond its role in movement, proprioception is fundamental in how our brain processes information from other sense organs.

Initially, this sense allowed the subject to quickly and precisely locate a potential danger in the environment, which helped ensure their survival. Proprioception is at the center of the neurological phenomena that make it possible to identify the source of sensory stimuli in space. It does not work independently but in connection with the other sense organs. It strongly influences their work by constantly giving the brain an indication of their respective places in the body.

The advantages of proprioception

Proprioception offers several benefits. Since it improves balance and posture, it benefits the elderly, people practicing tasks requiring repetitive movements daily, or athletes wishing to increase their performances.

But it can also serve another purpose. Try applying proprioception to a muscle-building session. For example, instead of taking a mat to do push-ups, take cushions or another object that will change your balance. Your muscles must adapt to find an adequate position to hold the posture to perform the requested exercise.

Another benefit of proprioception is the reduction and prevention of injuries. This technique seeks to strengthen the postural muscles, often in the abdominal belt, and can prevent back and spine pain. Good proprioception will allow the athlete to have better muscular control and, thus, improve their posture and coordination and know when they're well positioned, reducing stress on joints and muscles and limiting the risk of injury.

> Proprioception is a link between body and mind.

It will link the muscle and articulation system with the central nervous system on which inter- and intramuscular coordination depends. We must be aware that our musculoskeletal system, controlled by the central nervous system, works as a whole. The particularity of proprioceptive receptors is that they can act independently without the brain necessarily intervening. This is where our reflex movements come from, which is helpful to us when escaping danger, for example. A good proprioception is like a link between the muscles, the joints, and the central nervous system, allowing athletes to optimize their movement, running, jumping, landing, striking the ball, and other tasks while reducing their susceptibility to injury.

Examples of proprioception exercises

There's no need to go to the physiotherapist to practice proprioception. Most gyms are equipped with rollers or balance balls, which you can use to perform variations of your favorite exercises. The principle is to reduce the support surface of the body to make it work differently, thus improving balance.

Proprioceptive exercises are performed on the ground or with accessories like balance balls, platforms, and trampolines. Here are some simple examples:

• on an unstable surface (cushion or soft mat), stay balanced on one foot for one minute;

• run on the spot on a small trampoline, lifting your knees high;

• on an unstable platform, crouch and then get up slowly, trying to keep your balance;

• in a high-plank position, raise one hand and then the other. For more difficulty, try it with your hands on a small ball.

Our daily movement consists of analyzing signals from our different sense organs, which our brain processes continuously. The brain performs many tasks automatically, like balance management and breathing. These are fundamental to survival, allowing us to clear our minds and devote ourselves to higher-level cognitive activities.

However, the information coming from our sight, vestibular system, and proprioception must be concordant with the data of the immediate environment to allow the brain to process it correctly and function at its maximum capabilities. Otherwise, we would be in a state of vigilance and stress to verify the information and ensure survival: correctly identify the danger, do not fall, do not bump into it, etc.

When disturbed proprioception causes sensory conflicts, the brain can no longer process all the information from the other senses. This results in unconscious, temporary, and random visual information deletions appearing in certain gaze positions and when the subject receives auditory information.

Keep in mind that high levels of stress, anxiety, or anger can disturb the proprioception system.

Proprioception is a key element of orientation in everyday life, but even more so in sports, where it's essential to know the position and orientation of objects, partners, and opponents—and, above all, where your body is about them. Individuals' spatial orientation acts on two levels: a perceptual level, allowing the judgment of spatial orientation and verticality, and a motor level, allowing the achievement of vertical postural balance.

GIVING MEANING TO ELEMENTS WITH PERCEPTION

*****

Perception is a set of mechanisms by which we recognize, organize, and give meaning to the sensations we receive from environmental stimuli. It appeals to the five senses (mainly sight) and allows you to interact with the environment. Let's consider the perception-action cycle.

> Perception is the brain's construction of reality. The speed and precision with which athletes act, aim, catch, return, strike, and retaliate, the magic with which they keep their balance or perceive the slightest change in their environment, are due to well-developed sensory skills. Can we learn to have a more refined perception?

Yes, and it's called perceptual learning.

We can see in the visual field what we understand well, what we interpret correctly, and what we anticipate (more on the anticipation later).

Being observant is not fixing an object or an action but being able to process the correct information. In competition, there is a lot of information; some is relevant, but a lot isn't or is less so. In addition, all this information is distributed in a space that can be large and go beyond the anatomical limits of the visual system. These limits are related to the position of the eye and its functioning.

On one hand, the eye is in its orbit, protected by an arch, and limited in movement. On the other hand, the athlete must have the broadest possible vision. Their peripheral vision is imperfect but crucial for fast and precise movements. You must change the focal length quickly and move the visual beams in parallel.

Whatever the sport, athletes move their eyes subtly. Relevant information is processed in peripheral vision, which untrained individuals would have difficulty doing. Many would turn their heads. Top athletes must be able to use their peripheral vision while keeping their eyes focused on what's most important. They can do this because they know the situation well and what is likely to happen and can prepare accordingly.

SECTION 4 LUCIDITY IN THE ACTION

THE LIMITED ATTENTION

*****

Here is a conversation between the University of Asvana football coach, Jerry Mill, and one of his players, Duke Greyket, before the opening game of the 2019 season.

Mill: "If you want to win this match, be attentive and, above all, stay focused."

Duke: "Uhh, Coach, when should I be attentive?"

Mill: "Well, when you're not focused!"

Duke: "Yes, Coach, but to be focused and attentive, you always told me they don't have the same meaning, so I must be attentive to what? When? How? When should I focus on what? How? And, Coach, by the way, when do I have to be attentive? All the time? It's hard, Coach!"

Mill: "Er…." Then, he was silent for a moment. "It will be a little complicated if I explain to you. Stop with your questions, listen to what I tell you, don't think, and return to work if you want to succeed."

We often hear terms relating to attention, focus, and concentration in sports. All these elements play a crucial role in your capability to be lucid. But is there a difference between them?

As early as 1890, William James, one of the pioneers of psychology, defined attention as "the taking possession by the mind, in a clear and vivid form, of an object or a series of thoughts among several which seem possible.... It involves the removal of certain objects to treat others more effectively."

Attention is a selective mental orientation that increases efficiency in a particular activity mode and inhibits competing activities.

Attention is:

•   the information selector for consciousness;

•   a cerebral function that mobilizes our five senses and ensures the reception of information from our environment (visual or auditory messages or signals, tactile, gustatory, and olfactory).

But that's not all. It also lets us perceive what's happening inside us (feelings, emotions, our physiological state).

> Attention promotes the rapid and automatic perception and analysis of information. Thus, our attention can be drawn outward (e.g., to spectators' whistles, coaches' instructions, calls from teammates, etc.) or inward (e.g., to muscle pain, thoughts, high heart rate, etc.).

Attention is selective because individuals choose which elements to consider before acting. For example, before deciding to take a wave, a surfer's brain has access to a lot of information: the frequency and height of the waves, the orientation of the swell, the presence of a sandbank, the wind direction, the announcements of the scores, the position of opponents, the cheers of the crowd, the coach's recommendations, the intensity of the light and position of the sun, whether they've chosen the correct board or the correct tactic, muscle pain or nervous fatigue, even personal problems. For each action sought, the information available to the individual makes it impossible to consider and take charge of them entirely.

To be effective and meet the expectations of the example task (choosing a wave), the surfer must be able to choose by selecting information they deem helpful at that precise moment. The next logical step is to access and retain only the proper and most urgent information needed for accomplishing the task. Accessing less relevant information can cause poor performance. These disruptors are called distractions or distractors.

To sum up, we can say that attention allows us to perceive the information available before sorting it.

How do we apply selective thinking in competition?

During the competition, athletes must process a multitude of information via their five senses. They must quickly discern which data is necessary while sweeping away all the internal distractors (parasitic thoughts, cognitive and somatic manifestations of stress, anxiety, doubts, fears, etc.) and external distractors (weather, the opponent) that comprise a large part of their attentive resources. These distractions negatively influence the action to be performed.

How does our brain handle information processing?

In response to an internal or external stimulus, the brain must first absorb this mountain of information, select the most essential parts, process them, and finally return an answer.

Selective attention is an ability that everyone, regardless of their area of expertise and competence, must learn to master. It is probably the most critical cognitive characteristic of the victorious athlete; huge gaps exist between beginners, advanced athletes, and the elite. Contrary to what one might think, the mental difference between them is mainly in selecting information and not in the quantity of information processed. So, quality trumps quantity: The elite athlete is more efficient in getting to the point in information processing. Selective attention (like any other mental skill) is not innate but acquired by learning and training.

For example, ask a soccer player to take a penalty shot against a goalkeeper who moves strangely in front of them (their attention would be focused not on the goalkeeper but on the pivot foot and then the surface of the foot used for striking). Have an archer shoot with music they dislike playing loudly in the background. You get the idea: Anything to distract them!

Always remember: Attention is limited.

In psychology, the Stroop Effect refers to the interference observed between a primary task and an interfering cognitive process. For example, let's say your task is to name a color in which a word is written, but the word itself is the name of another color (such as the word orange written in blue ink). The interference you experience while trying not to read the word as written is the Stroop Effect.

We have limited information-processing capacity. Attention requires effort and consumes more or less energy depending on the object of attention, the context, and, above all, the individual. Attention corresponds to a limited capacity for processing information. Indeed, each person's ability to process stimuli is different. This is called the individual's attentional capacity.

This consideration implies that the different mental and motor tasks require a limited information-processing space. If a task mobilizes the entire processing space, all the available attention is fixed on it, to the detriment of other tasks. On the other hand, if all the space is not fully used, the individual can perform different tasks. This is referred to as the selective-attention-capacity model. Anyone wishing to carry out a task correctly must know how to direct their attention to perform it efficiently. Why? Because our information-processing system is limited in capacity, it is sometimes difficult to control everything simultaneously.

To develop their attention, the athlete must learn to:

• anticipate the selection of relevant information (more on this in the last part of the book);

• identify and control distraction factors (generated by stress, fatigue, and the competitive environment);

• recognize the focus modes necessary for the task and know how to switch effectively from one focus mode to another.

For example, in football, when the team does not have the ball, a defender can be attentive to their attacker, their placement, or a specific field area, according to the context of the moment. Then, they must be attentive to other elements when their team regains possession, and they must do this as quickly as possible, especially when playing at higher levels.

Just as you or I can drive a car while simultaneously activating the turn signal, looking in the rearview mirror, and talking to a passenger, a tennis player must consider the trajectory and spin of the ball as it approaches them while choosing a racket grip and type and placement of their return shot. This is called the automation of the gesture. The more a subject masters the execution of a motor gesture, the less they need to maintain their attention, allowing them to direct their attention to other factors to optimize their response.

Thus, an individual who cannot perform an automated gesture must not simultaneously focus on too much external and secondary information.

This leads to cognitive overload and loss of lucidity, which sometimes generates stress or anxiety (cognitive and/or somatic) or sometimes simply mental and/or physical fatigue, thus hindering performance.

Knowing how to use attentional resources best and not wasting them by focusing on unuseful or parasitic information (physical pain, negative thoughts, referee errors, howls from a spectator) requires specific training and practice. If a mental trainer can propose this work, these notions of selective attention also concern other stakeholders, such as trainers, teachers, educators, and parents. However, for anyone who asks the individual to consider information that exceeds their processing capacity, the outcome will likely be the failure to carry out the task asked.

FLEXIBLE AND ORIENTABLE ATTENTION

*****

What's the fundamental difference between the competitive sports of yesterday and today?

SPEED.

Game speed, reaction speed, gesture speed, movement speed, information-processing speed, comprehension speed, decision speed—everything is faster now. Prodigious scientific progress has aided speed in various performance-determining fields, such as physical preparation, biomechanics, technological innovation, and dietetics.

Imagine organizing tennis matches between Björn Borg, Yannick Noah, Ivan Lendl, Pete Sampras, Roger Federer, and the world No. 1 in 2030. How about a hypothetical football tournament between Real Madrid in 1960, Ajax Amsterdam in 1974, AC Milan in 1989, Real Madrid in 2002, FC Barcelona in 2011, and the winner of the Champions League in 2030—who would win?

The athlete who can best respond to the speed of modern sport is the one who can open their five senses to receive, process, sort, and select the information that is useful and relevant to the successful completion of a task. They can also quickly reject useless or parasitic information, which allows them to remain open to other external parameters.

Attention is selective and limited, but it's also flexible, orientable, and therefore perfectible through training tailored to the task and the athlete's skill level.

Here's a challenge: Watch a football game and try to count the number of players on the same half of the field. At the same time, pay attention to your breathing by observing your stomach swelling and deflating with each breath.

Successful challenge? If not, don't panic—it's normal. While your brain can process, sort, select, and retain a lot of information simultaneously, it cannot focus on two different attention fields simultaneously.

Indeed, your attention has two dimensions:

• The extent of the attention can be broad (the athlete considers a large number of sensory information) or narrow (he selects one or two precise sensory information). To put it simply, it works a bit like a camera zoom.

• The direction of attention can be external (directed toward an external object like a ball or a wave) or internal (centered on themselves, like the position of their arm in the execution of a gesture). The internal-external continuum is also called associative-dissociative. The athlete associates the sensations they perceive with their task or dissociates these two parameters by focusing on external aspects, which can act as distractions.

These two independent parameters thus define four modes of attentional focusing:

• internal/wide (turned toward you but to seek no tactical solution);

• internal/narrow (self-directed, kinesthetic sensations);

• external/broad (perception of information);

• external/narrow (fixing of a precise point—the zoom);

While the human brain is capable of extraordinary prowess, there are actions it cannot perform. If a motor task requires alternate modes, we can't simultaneously direct our attention to two distinct modes of focus. An athlete needs to acquire maximum attentional flexibility.

To illustrate this point, imagine a player taking a free kick in football: Once they've placed the ball and have backed away to gain momentum, they look at the placement of the opponents' wall, their teammates, and the goalkeeper (external/wide); then they decide on a strategy to execute their strike (internal/wide) while perhaps taking deep breaths to recover from the past action (a gesture that can be automated). Then, they can motivate themselves with positive internal dialogue (internal/narrow) while looking at the precise place where they want to place the ball (external/narrow). Lastly, they gesture while the opposing goalkeeper detects the information necessary to stop the shot.

Attentional strategies and relevant information to consider when carrying out a task vary according to the sport (open/closed skills, environmental uncertainties, etc.) and the athlete's level of practice. However, regardless of discipline, an athlete must learn to direct and quickly change the extent and direction of their attention depending on the task at hand.

In competition, the level of stress, distraction, and physiological and mental activation are all elements that can shake the focus of the athlete's attention. An athlete with efficient concentration and attention for their performance has excellent attentional flexibility, which means they can orient and use their five senses to the four modes of attentional focus according to demand, context, and moment of the task.

In conclusion, it is essential for an athlete, student, employee, or any person carrying out a particular task to learn to work their attentional flexibility. Among other things, they will:

• learn to identify valuable information for carrying out the task;

• automate certain gestures and actions to free attentional resources (master ball handling so you can direct your attention to the ball calls of your partners);

• control the internal distraction factors (project your thoughts into the future while considering the result and the next match; negative internal dialogue and parasitic thoughts like thinking that we are going to miss the action; thinking about the past, their physical pain, to their tiredness ... like, for example, to say that one has never beaten their opponent or that one is tired);

• recognize the modes of attention necessary for the different actions;

• quickly and efficiently switch from one focusing mode to another;

• remain stoic in the face of trash-talking. For example, in tennis, John McEnroe's antics were sometimes used to distract his opponent when he needed a boost, allowing him to refocus.

It is crucial to know where to focus your attention. When you feel you're not controlling a situation, you try to focus on everything. By planning, you can eliminate the risk of being overwhelmed.

ATTENTIONAL FOCUS

*****

Since our attention is limited, we can't be aware of all the parameters of our experience simultaneously. Choosing what to focus our attention on first is called attentional focus.

Some athletes may have a biased attentional focus. They tend to focus only on certain aspects of reality and ignore others. For example, anxious people may focus on the threatening and dangerous elements of the future. Athletes with depression often focus their attention on the imperfect and negative aspects of themselves, others, and the world.

Focusing attention on threatening aspects may cause an anxious person to avoid new situations because of fear of danger, preventing them from enjoying the present moment.

For the person suffering from depression, focusing constantly on the negative aspects deprives them of hope. It reinforces the feeling of helplessness, thus limiting any action aimed at changing things or engaging in pleasant activities.

The attentional focus has significant impacts on three levels:

- Perceiving and making sense of a situation (cognitive)
- Reacting to it emotionally (emotion)
- The motivation and behavior of the person (behavior)

Attentional focus influences two essential parameters: our emotional well-being and having functional or limiting behaviors.

Attentional focus can change in two ways: automatically (a noise or a movement attracts our attention) or voluntarily (I decide to return my attention to my running when I catch myself daydreaming about my next vacation in the Madeira Islands).

We have power over our attentional focus and two levers of action: We can influence it voluntarily or learn to focus on specific characteristics of our sport automatically.

Distractions are plentiful on the athletic field, both in training and even more so in competition. Whether it is external distractions (a shout in the audience, the arrival of a loved one on the edge of the field, an adverse reaction from a teammate, a referee's error) or internal distractions (fear, stress, negative thoughts, evil—or even good—feelings), they can ultimately take you out of what you have to do in the present moment.

So, how do you keep yourself entirely focused?

This question arises at any level, from the beginner who has to store a great deal of information during their first few hours of practice to the expert who is subjected to pressures that monopolize their attention.

How can we process all the information that our brain constantly receives and consider only that which is helpful during training or competition?

Attention is a finite resource allocated to particular objects or mental events (sensations, thoughts, emotions) rather than others.

What attentional problems does an athlete face in training and competition?

First, managing your attentional effort over time can be difficult. In some sports, the athlete must maintain vigilance for long, sometimes hours. In others, the attentional effort is brief but repeated. Fatigue makes it even more difficult.

The second problem is deciding which problem to focus on. Attentional focus can be of different types: internal (heart rate), external (visual cues), on the gesture (the action of grouping in a somersault, for example), or the result (the target and trajectory of the ball).

Since the early 1990s, researchers in sports psychology have been comparing the effectiveness of these different types of attentional focus but have yet to reach an absolute consensus. Indeed, the efficacy of these other focuses would depend on the nature of the task, the level of expertise, and the preferences of each athlete. In addition, the world's top athletes use several attentional focuses (in limited numbers) to prepare and carry out the same action.

The third attention problem for athletes is difficulty staying focused on these attentional focuses when the distractions are too strong.

The athlete will then allocate attentional resources to unimportant things, diverting them from relevant information. An emotion like stress, fear, joy, or shame can grab an athlete's attention, and in athletics, where everything is played out in a few thousandths of a second, that slightest deviation in focus can be fatal.

So, how do you optimize the attention of athletes?

Recent research shows that we can better regulate our attention, thus limiting these problems and their deleterious effects on learning and performance.

So, attentional focus is defined as a mental skill that can be developed, like physical, technical, or tactical skills.

Before attention training, the first questions to ask yourself are:

- What is the nature of attentional effort in my sport?

- How long is it?

- What is its intensity?

- Does it vary throughout the game?

- Is it distributed attention because the environment is constantly changing in an unpredictable way (e.g., the football player who has to consider several pieces of information at the same time, such as the ball, position of opponents, partners, etc.) or focused attention in a stable and specific environment (e.g., the archer focused on the target)?

Train your attention as you train a physical quality

From there, you can verify that your training allows for the same attentional effort required in competition.

For example, a show-jumping rider who trains for two hours may have difficulty putting forth the right attentional effort in a competition that lasts only a minute or two. Therefore, care must be taken to train their attention while respecting the specificities of their sport and the context of competition. As in physical preparation, to maintain a specific type of attentional effort in competition, sometimes you must take on higher attentional loads. This may include setting up situations in training where attentional effort must be maintained twice as long as in the competition situation or overloading the athlete with information to be processed.

Defining attentional anchors

At the same time, the coach must be able to define precisely what the athlete should pay attention to, giving them simple and relevant instructions for improving their attentional focus. These attentional focuses must be seen as anchors that will allow the athlete to find their way back to their attention if they get lost in a surplus of thoughts. It is preferable to define these focuses and that they have specific meaning for the athlete above all. They must also make sense of the work in progress and the degree of acquisition of one's skills.

Motivation, an attention channel

The most motivated athletes usually have fewer attention problems.

Indeed, when we know precisely why we are training and are determined to achieve our goal, it becomes apparent that we must stay focused on the task and give it all our attention. So, by setting goals that arouse interest, represent a challenge, and are achievable, we promote an optimal state of attention. You will then make sure to define a clear objective for each competition, each match, each session, and even each exercise. The effect of motivation on the athlete's attention will be all the more important as the athlete defines their goal and the means to achieve it.

CONCENTRATION IS A MENTAL SKILL OF PERFORMANCE.

*****

Concentration consists of focusing on relevant information from the environment and yourself and keeping it focused for as long as it takes. It serves as a protection mechanism for the attention to resist all the distracting parasitic thoughts. Instead of favoring the reception of sensory signals (noises, sounds, etc.) emanating from the environment, the process of concentration blocks the arrival of our awareness of any stimulation that may disturb our mind.

In summary, concentration is the ability to focus on what matters (task and environment) and the time necessary to accomplish the task (technical gesture, observation of external elements, etc.).

Thus, the concentration:

• is sustained attention that nothing interrupts and which varies according to the difficulty of the task to be performed;

• allows you to use your working memory to receive, search, select, and process relevant information.

• promotes the use of mental or thinking mechanisms.

Concentration has several components, including attention. Attention is like the light beam of a flashlight, which means that it must be aimed at specific locations to allow better performance. Depending on the sport and the situation, the focus of attention can be narrow or wide, like the beam of a lamp.

The second component is the ability to optimize physical intensity. Too much intensity narrows the focus and causes what is commonly called "tunnel vision." A narrow focus harms performance in team sports like hockey or football. In addition, excessive intensity causes muscle tension and affects the coordination and fluidity of finesse movements. It is necessary to keep an appropriate intensity, depending on the sport and the situation, to optimize concentration.

A third essential component of concentration is the ability to block distractions. As the human being has a limited capacity for processing information, it is necessary to know how to block unnecessary details and focus on the elements critical to performance. This implies a knowledge of the elements essential to performance. Mistakes, worries, anger, expectations, spectators, and nervousness are all sources of potential distractions that can affect concentration. An important factor to consider is fatigue. The more tired an athlete is, the harder it will be for them to focus on the performance essentials. So, good physical condition is necessary for good concentration.

Another important component of concentration is the ability to control thoughts. This means maintaining a positive attitude and thinking about what you must do rather than the results.

It is essential to have confidence in your abilities and to cultivate positive thoughts because negative thoughts often become a source of distraction and cause overanalysis. In most sports, it is better to keep things simple and not analyze too much because there is a risk of analytical paralysis. Finally, the athlete must recognize the elements under their control and not expend mental energy on what is beyond their control.

The last major component of concentration is the ability to refocus when distracted. Even if athletes do their best to minimize distractions, they are sometimes unavoidable. It is necessary to identify the sources of potential distractions and plan a refocus strategy.

Focusing is a passive art. If you try too hard to concentrate, you can lose your concentration! You must free your brain and let your training take over.

In sports, we see variations in athletes' attention: Boxers forget to protect themselves during fights, cyclists forget to pedal, basketball players seem to forget simple instructions repeated many times in training, and gymnasts lose track of their sequences—the list is endless. Athletes must be present, engaged, and sure to think of salient activity elements to carry out their action plan.

High-level competition demands even more and does not support the slightest loophole, relaxation, or deviation because the sanction is immediate.

Archery requires an extreme amount of attention. Current competition standards have reduced the number of arrows fired, and the slightest gap at the high international level is heavily penalized. Attentional fluctuations of an archer are at the heart of the discipline.

"There are no badly shot arrows; there are only badly prepared arrows," said the two-time U.S. Olympic champion Darrell Pace.

What is selective concentration?

Concentration is the ability to focus one's attention on a specific goal. For archery strategy, this means focusing on what is essential, which is the center of the target.

We often hear coaches on the shooting range imploring their archers to "concentrate." But what exactly should they concentrate on?

The archer arrives carrying their bow and positions themselves before the target. Then, they place their fingers on the string and the other hand on the bow's handle, which they put in light tension. They align their forearm with the arrow. Then, pulling their arm back, they stretch the string as far as possible and gently place the arrow and the bow at the level of the target they are staring at. Finally, they let go of the rope. The arrow flies toward the target as the bow arm releases from its tension, pulling the bow down. Its successful execution requires physical strength, skill, and excellent concentration.

That's a lot to concentrate on! In a competitive context with significant stress, archers must concentrate on themselves and detach from the result. Because, let's face it, some things (the wind, the brightness, the talent of the competitors) are out of their control. The archers must focus both on themselves and the target.

Archery performance relies on technical, physical, and mental abilities. The cognitive domain includes, among others, concentration. It corresponds to the ability to focus on a specific point. In the learning phase, attention to a single technical element of the shooting is privileged, while very often, with expertise, the archer can use different points of attention (attentional fluctuations). The archer aims to produce the highest quality shooting technique with each arrow.

Archery training consists of repeating the same gesture with precision. Attention to a particular technical shooting element is used during each training session to strengthen the archer's mastery of movement. In competition, the archer often selects the most crucial aspect of their shot and seeks to focus their attention on it from the first to the last arrow. Archers sometimes encounter difficulties maintaining the same quality of attention, generally followed by a degradation of the gesture and, therefore, of the performance.

Consequently, the challenge is to determine indicators for the archer and the trainer that allow anticipation of the degradation of attention, which is not always sanctioned immediately by the performance but can very quickly have repercussions if the archer does not respond. In this sense, it appears essential to identify and characterize these moments to define and implement strategies to allow the archer to continue their performance.

Examples:

The archer focuses on pulling the rope (technical element) by focusing on the sensation of muscular effort produced by the fixing muscles of the scapula, emphasizing the median trapezius.

The archer focuses on the pulling of the rope (technical element) by initially focusing on the recoil of the elbow in space and then on the sensation of muscular effort or the permanent recoil of the rope.

Absence versus presence

Sometimes, archers feel they are not paying attention to a particular point, which you might call "attentional absence." If, on the one hand, it frees the automatisms, it can generate harmful effects when the archer realizes their absence and tries to refocus their attention. This is how we could evoke a state of concentration that refers to what is being done, being felt and observed, and which places the archer in action here and now, without elements linked to the past or future.

Presence can be considered from different angles since it can cause focus on one or more technical aspects. Archers verbalize certain states by asserting that they were "thinking of nothing," which translates into a generalist focus reflecting the same dispersion. Moving toward relaxation, for example, is a performance-seeking position because it lowers attentional costs. It can be a step in the search for their generalist attentional state.

Shoot your arrows rather than let go.

Behind this expression hides a drastic difference in commitment; the archer must remain an actor in what he does rather than enduring the action with doubts. Although sometimes the notion of letting go can take on the idea of relaxation or tension, the shooter must be willful and determined in their shot.

Go until the end

The archer must fight against attentional fluctuations and not lose concentration while shooting the last few arrows. This can also be applied to the archer who tends to systematically focus on the arrow's impact on the target by forgetting to finish their shot, mainly by not using proper postural stability and getting the visual needed to shoot a good arrow.

Exhibit more amplitude

With fatigue, the shot becomes less fluid, the elbow does not move back, and the tension exerted on the string by the shooter changes. This has fewer repercussions on the arrow's trajectory (the tension exerted determines the speed and the trajectory). This instruction is often used when the shooter, over time, tends to tense up and reduce their actions. Regarding engagement at the start, the archer must maintain the pulling force of the rope and their postural stability.

Do not rush

In the emotion of the action, archers may tend to skip specific steps in their preparation or rush to complete them. It is the recovery phase—or the quality of execution—that suffers. In particular, the phases of placing and finding balance at the start of shooting are degraded, even though they condition the end of shooting. To fight against this tendency, it is advisable to ask the athlete to synchronize themselves by paying their attention to the planned protocols, which are integrated: the positioning of the feet, the fingers on the rope, and the breathing (take a deep breath and exhale slowly while seeking a form of muscular and attentional relaxation).

Take time between arrows.

Throughout the competition, the tendency is to reduce recovery time and lengthen the shooting times. This tendency is due to a lack of recoil in the action; the archer focuses on what seems essential (shooting), forgetting that they can only be effective if they are well prepared. Asking the archer to take their time stimulates them so that they can maintain their release and preparation routines.

Staying on it

That means continuing to maintain attention on the target, even after the arrow has launched; the tendency of the shooter in a hurry to see their result is to break the fluidity of the rope release and shift their head to check the impact on the target. It isn't suitable for the trajectory when it happens too early.

Sort the information

The archer is constantly subjected to a large flow of information that he must sort through; otherwise, he will be overwhelmed. Sometimes, the athlete's sensitivity prompts them to process information that obscures the most important. Sorting out consists of focusing on what is essential for the performance and trying to evacuate what is not, especially about the shooting protocol.

Refocus on a simple skill.

When the archer is overwhelmed by information about their shooting routine and external elements such as the wind or the opponent's score, they can become "lost." They can no longer make simple and effective decisions. Refocusing on a simple skill means restricting oneself to staying in an operational, functional, automated mode to find simplicity and fluidity in the shooting.

Aim for your zone

Aiming corresponds to a frame fixed in advance by the archer and consists of delimiting an impact zone as a functional benchmark.

For example, by setting an area up to eight (red on the target) as an objective, the shooter does not focus on the 10 (the bull' s-eye). They remain in a smooth shooting position because they can hit eight effortlessly. Focusing their attentional energy on the 10 could be too intense and likely cause negative feedback each time they fail to hit the bull' s-eye.

Leave the result aside.

This recommendation pertains to the athlete's results and the results of their teammates or opponents. Worrying about results may cause them to leave their routine, not remain in the moment, and move away from the practical modalities inherent in acting. It's like a crucial free throw in basketball near the end of a game: If the shooter can't escape the importance of whether or not they make the shot, it can disrupt their routine, making the simple gesture much more complex. Leaving the result aside is asking the archer to stop worrying about impacts and to focus on the actual technical methods of shooting.

Demobilization

Demobilization refers to a break in the state of engagement. The athlete is no longer invested enough in their action, reflected in their lack of conviction in their execution routines; the archer is not mentally locked in because an element kept them away from it. It can be very time-bound but can even cause the athlete to quit the competition.

Shoot all your arrows.

"Shoot all your arrows" refers to the arrows' demand for attention over time, from the first to the last. The archer must retain their concentration for the entire time, not focusing too much on any one arrow. They must remain present and attentive throughout the series.

Commit to the end

It also ensures, in a more localized manner, that the archer does not weaken on the last shots, which are characterized by more marked, even cumulative fatigue and an eagerness to finish because one may believe that the results are frozen and the rankings acquired. Wanting to stay in the present is an effort to keep the archer in peak condition to perform well.

What is good archery performance?

Of course, it's a sport, so we are constantly looking for performance quantified in points gained by hitting the target. But "shooting well" can have a different meaning. It can refer to the technical principles of shooting: posture, dynamics, relaxation, fluidity, and continuity in the movement. Good performance depends on staying in the present and avoiding falling into the traps of anticipation or feedback. Anticipation consists of projecting oneself further in the firing sequences in time: to be eager to finish, to be tempted to access a selective phase for the finals or to reach a personal best.

This projection is essential for the motivational sphere. Still, on the other hand, in the action, it is necessary that the archer remains present and focused on the shooting of each arrow. Similarly, retro-projecting consists of going back and dwelling on an earlier miscue, and the consequences caused by this lack of concentration can be crippling to performance.

CLARITY/PERSPICUITY

*****

Learning to release your thoughts is important for having a clear and precise mind. It helps stimulate creativity, increase alertness, and increase concentration.

Why do you have to learn to release your thoughts?

Have you ever had your mind overloaded so you couldn't handle everything?

Try the following eight tips to free your thinking and to have clear and precise ideas.

1. Having a clear mind requires emptying your brain.

The principle here is to eliminate everything from your mind. This is very useful when you want to organize your life; we often procrastinate or feel overwhelmed by our thoughts and tasks.

Who is the brain drain for?

For everyone, it is significant if you recognize yourself in these situations:

• You don't know where to start;

• you want to plan your days, but your head is full;

• you think about too many things at once;

• You go from one task to another without being effective, which exhausts you all day.

So, how do you empty your brain?

Several methods are beautiful: You choose what works for you. You need a place to write (pen and paper or an application), a moment to do it, and good conditions. The key here is to make it a habit. Whether it's every day or every week, it's a great tool.

It's up to you to choose what you want—test some methods before committing to one. Here's how I drain my brain.

I do two sessions: one every day and one per week or month, depending on my needs and state of mind. For my daily brain drain, here's how I do it:

Before bed, I grab my legal pad called BRAINDUMP each evening. Inside, things are inscribed: these are all the tasks I have not yet assigned, arranged, or finalized. At that moment, I think about what pollutes my mind and what I don't want to forget and add them to the list. It takes me between two and five minutes.

It's swift because if I do it regularly and because nothing pollutes my head too much. Also, if I think of something during the day, I'll add it to the list.

The next step (only if I have more than five or 10 minutes) is to review the list with all my tasks. Three actions are possible:

1. Do: If the task takes less than five minutes, I complete it and do as much as possible during the time dedicated to brain drain that day.

2. Plan: I plan one or more tasks for the next day.

3. Delete or delegate: If I see something that does not speak to me or that I no longer want, I either delete it or delegate it to someone else. This allows me to move on, sort my list, and focus my time on things that matter.

My weekly session is often longer, which can happen when I feel overwhelmed or know I must organize the following week. For example, I will take 30 to 60 minutes to plan my business and personal week and empty my brain simultaneously. After looking at my brain-drain list, I can assign and prioritize things to do while clearing my mind.

The most important thing is to find out what works and use it. Don't turn it into another to-do list that complicates your life. To help you clear your brain (if you're feeling stuck, know that you have things to note but don't know where to start), here are some questions to ask yourself:

- Are there things that worry me right now?

- Is there something I must do that I always forget to do?

- What do I always leave aside and would like to finish?

- Is there an upcoming event or occasion that's important?

- Do you need to make a phone call or see someone soon?

- Is there something important that you have wanted to do for a long time but never planned?

- What would make you happy?

Make your brain drain as you feel it. The main thing is to first empty the drawers before sorting to feel more serene.

2. Take a walk.

Taking a walk is a great way to improve the quality of your thinking. Go outside and breathe deeply through your nose. You will get a good dose of oxygen for your brain, and the change of scenery can help clear your mind.

3. Make room for your thoughts.

No one can act correctly when their thoughts are out of order. Organizing your physical workspace means that your mind will not wander when you have made room for clear thinking.

4. Sleep better.

Sleep requirements are variable, but the minimum required for most is seven hours.

It has been reported that people suffer when they sleep less than seven hours. Research says sleep quality is essential for brain function after a certain minimum quota.

5. Try meditation.

Short on time? Close your eyes, relax, and watch your breath for a while. Accept your mind wandering and focus on your breathing again.

6. Resolve any irritations of the mind.

Observe things bothering you and do something to rid yourself of them. For example, make that phone call you've been putting off or make a to-do list, and your mind will go free for a moment.

7. Make decisions quickly

Nothing interferes with clear thinking, like making a dozen decisions simultaneously. Take it one step at a time, one decision at a time.

8. Meet your physical needs

Clear thinking happens more easily when you're not too hungry, thirsty, hot, cold, tired, etc.

There are more than eight ways to release your thinking, but trying a few techniques will help you have a clearer mind. The most important things are to be serene and to flourish in your life. Consider all aspects of your life and try to find a balance between each area.

> When you feel exhausted mentally and physically, take time for yourself. This anxiety and lack of mental clarity tell us that we have accumulated thoughts, emotions, and doubts that we cannot release. We must let them go so our minds can reset and regain balance.

HOW DO WE APPRAISE A SITUATION?

*****

In some sports, situational awareness and quick and accurate decision-making are paramount. These essential skills for optimal performance can be significantly improved by specific cognitive-perceptual training that would improve:

• analyzing the situation and maintaining tactical control during a match;

• adaptation to an emergency and the adversary;

• visual tracking of moving objects and anticipating trajectories;

• controlling emotions; remaining calm under stress or pressure;

• peripheral vision, thus avoiding shocks or tackles in team sports.

Below, we present four innovative cognitive sports training tools that are easy to access, download, and install with just a few clicks.

• NeuroTracker (Canada, neurotracker.net)

NeuroTracker, a virtual system used by FC Barcelona, Manchester United, and Olympique Lyonnais, allows athletes to optimize their perceptual and cognitive abilities.

It is an immersive 3D training system designed to isolate and train the attentional mechanisms associated with vision. This workout increases the speed of analyzing a visual scene, increases concentration duration, and strengthens the ability to moderate emotional responses.

- Intelligym (USA, intelligym.com)

Intelligym was designed for Air Force pilots by DARPA (Defense Advanced Research Projects Agency).

Major NHL, NBA, and some US national teams use it as a training tool. The application is very accessible and easy to install and use. It's accompanied by brief online training and presented as a simplified video game.

This tool is based on the research of Professor Daniel Gopher, an expert in cognitive science.

Its use can improve cognitive abilities by approximately 30 percent.

Downloadable on tablets and smartphones, Intelligym is specific to team sports and simulates game actions to develop attention, decision-making, peripheral vision, and other things. Though it may look like a video game, this application should not be confused with one. It is a fundamental field tool designed to engage the athlete's brain in a targeted manner. It can be used on the computer and projected onto a television screen.

- NeuroNation (France, neuronation.fr) and Peak (USA, peak.net)

Like Peak, the NeuroNation app was developed by neuroscientists to develop cognition.

This free smartphone app includes games that stimulate memory, focus, and logic. Less specific than Intelligym or NeuroTracker, these two apps can easily find their place in your toolbox. At the coach's request, athletes can download it to their phones several times a week. Coaches can check progress and make good decisions quickly. The games correspond to categories of exercises: mental agility, concentration, attention, reasoning, memory, and even emotions.

The advantages of these two applications lie in their simplicity and ability to monitor progress in real-time.

What are the best ways to use these tools?

• Determine athletes' needs (attention, peripheral vision, reasoning skills).

• Plan sessions within the training cycle but outside of technical or physical sessions.

• Plan exercises within specific technical or physical sessions.

The goal here is to develop the athlete's cognitive abilities in a situation (during a session) despite fatigue or pressure. For example, during a period of rest during strength/explosiveness sessions, performing a cognitive exercise of your choice (decision-making, attention).

DECISION MAKING: DECISIVENESS

*****

Whether local competitions or large international competitions for which mentality, anticipation, and decision-making determine qualities, cognitive training provides a profound key to optimizing these qualities. Indeed, tools such as NeuroTracker have proven their effectiveness in terms of training, suggesting a promising future for their type of program in amateur or professional sports structures.

Regarding transferability acquired in a sports field, several researchers in cognition and neuroscience agree that this is possible.

The tactical skills of athletes, which require decision-making, are a determining factor in performance and expertise in sport. Athletes are good at recognizing and using meaningful information in sporting situations. They respond to the problems posed by competition by choosing the appropriate responses.

These decision-making skills must also be distinguished from technical skills. Thus, an athlete can have good technical skills without the ability to choose an adequate response at the right time. Training should judiciously combine the development of tactical and technical skills.

Decision-making training combines technical training, tactical training, and physical effort to improve long-term performance under competitive conditions. It aims to develop the decision-making process during training sessions. Beyond an increased cognitive effort in athletes, the desired effects are: (a) better retention and better long-term transfer of technical-tactical skills in competition, (b) better decision-making capacity and problem-solving in the athlete in competition, and (c) a greater capacity for autonomy and self-analysis of performance.

The first step concerns the analysis of the athletic task. It consists of identifying the cognitive activities of the athlete in a competitive situation, such as the best information focused on, which index to use to anticipate, and how to recover a memory best to solve a problem.

The second step is to identify and develop exercises or a sequence of exercises to train the cognitive processes of the previous step.

The tools:

1. Video modeling consists of using video recordings as educational support. The athlete can see a peer to learn what needs to be done. It can be a "model" to master the skill at different levels. The important thing is that the athlete can analyze the performance to be achieved.

2. Variable training involves variations in the parameters (amplitude, speed, etc.) of the same skill or of a motor program to cover different sports situations that are representative of competitions.

3. Random training calls for combining different skills in the same sequence to simulate real competition conditions.

4. Video feedback. As in the case of video modeling, video is used as educational support. It allows the athlete to see what is being done well and what needs to be corrected.

5. Questioning requires the coach to question the athlete to check their understanding and stimulate their cognitive effort by identifying information relevant to decision-making.

Decision-making training is a training approach that can positively contribute to improving athletic performance.

It is commonly accepted that a process involves a series of operations leading to a result. How can we describe, explain, and understand these operations when we are making a decision in a game or sports situation? The praxeological approach refuses to consider the player as the toy of the game but as a decision-maker who takes advantage of the difficulties involved. Motor praxeology places the praxis decision at the forefront of physical and sports activities.

Step 1: Define the decisions you need to make when competing

• Define the cognitive skills necessary to perform at a high level.

Example of seven cognitive skills in alpine skiing:

• anticipation: respond to the ski slope (terrain, pace, speed);

• concentration: focus on the task;

• attention: choose the correct track to take before or during the performance (inspection);

• recognition: recognize the patterns of objects while skiing quickly;

• recalling: recalling lived situations;

• problem-solving: solving problems in a known or new environment;

• decision-making: multiple situations and under pressure.

Step 2: Identify and describe the exercise or activity that best leads to decision-making

• Appropriate for the athlete's level of development

Example of alpine skiing:

• Create a safe environment that allows for maximum decision-making

Step 3: Choose one or more of the tools from Step 1 that best support training in decision-making.

Several approaches can be considered at the decision-making level. Praxeology pertains specifically to a motor decision, which would be a motor behavior manifesting in its accomplishment a choice linked to the uncertainty of a situation. Your decision presents the originality of taking shape in motor behavior during the flow of the action and participating immediately in the resolution of a motor task.

Similarly, the ecological approach will consider the decision-making process as an integral component of the goal-directed behavior of the individual, influenced by the functional constraints of the relationship between the individual and their environment. The cognitive approach will focus on the different stages of information processing. It will differentiate, in particular, the stages of judgment and decision-making. Judgment is supposed to represent a set of evaluative and inferential processes that individuals have at their disposal and can rely on in making decisions. Their process is separate from the consequences of the decision itself. A decision is defined by the acts or the options from which an individual must choose, by the implications and possible results of these acts, and by the elements that condition the relationship between the consequence and the acts.

These different approaches all offer a fascinating insight into decision-making.

Here is an example of how it works in team sport:

1. Presentation

Imagine a handball player approaching the opposing goal with the ball in hand in an attacking situation...

2. Identification

...they will try to identify from situations they have already encountered in training or previous matches whether or not the move they're thinking of implementing worked.

3. Generation

About their previous knowledge, the player will start to generate options...

4. Consideration

...they will consider them according to their value about the situation, then...

5. Selection

...they will select the option they deem most appropriate in their situation, e.g., pass to the left winger.

6. Execution

The next step corresponds to the driving realization that the player has selected the option, then...

7. Evaluation

... In the end, the player will evaluate both the option he has chosen and the quality of their execution before finding a new game configuration that presents itself to them.

This option-generation model will enable an understanding of cognitive functioning based on heuristics. A heuristic is a mental process, conscious or unconscious, which ignores some information and whose use in athletes has been shown in previous studies.

In particular, the option generation model served as the basis for the "Take-the-First" heuristic, which says to choose the first option that comes to mind. This heuristic is theoretically also the best if one has a certain degree of expertise and familiarity with the task under consideration. About individual differences, Take-the-First has been linked to intuition in the field of sport.

Intuition is the brain's ability to offer us information without consciously creating a path of reflection. It is to listen to what your brain spontaneously provides you as an answer.

Those who do not listen to their intuition will seek to develop answers voluntarily and will waste time. The solution to deciding quickly is to learn to listen to the responses, which are the spontaneous actions of the brain.

Please note: The more spontaneous an action, the more it will be linked to emotional states and the less rational it will be. Contrary to what one might think, an intuition may be worse than a carefully considered decision. But in an emergency, you must be able to count on these intuitions to facilitate your decision-making.

An adequate reaction is a follow-up reaction. Even if your brain has analyzed the situation regarding your objectives and quickly determined the best automation to use, it still needs to be able to inform you of this choice.

Even though most studies based on the option-generation model focus on aspects of generation, consideration, and selection (the "what"), it is essential not to neglect the motor-execution phase of the decision (the "how").

Emotions influence the cognitive performance of athletes, particularly decision-making performance.

Recent research has shown that emotions affect decision-making, not whether the feelings are positive or negative in their hedonic tone but through the physiological dimension and heart rate variability.

Practical application points

• Introduce relaxation activities (yoga, meditation, slow, controlled breathing, etc.) within the training to increase parasympathetic activity, which consequently increases performance in decision-making in the field.

• Systematically work on decision-making in training (for example, in attack situations in team sports) by establishing pressure conditions, which will help immunize against the pressure by adapting the parasympathetic system.

As an example, we can associate decision-making exercises with immediate consequences. Let's say a player misses an action; we can associate a personal negative consequence (such as running laps or doing push-ups in front of the rest of the team) or a collective negative consequence (the whole team does laps or push-ups). It's up to the coach, depending on the situation.

• Evaluate athletes' differences to detect who is more sensitive to a significant drop in parasympathetic activity under pressure, particularly with emotional intelligence.

Likewise, assessing athletes' tendency for intuition and deliberation would help identify those who ask too many questions. Athletes showing low emotional intelligence or a tendency to deliberate may thus be the subject of a specific intervention.

Elite athletes have a bank of game situations stored in their explicit memory, declarative memory. This is the conscious long-term memory that is easily and intentionally recalled. In addition, athletes have garnered numerous gaming situations automatically and unconsciously in their implicit memory, which provides them with adapted and rapid reactions.

What is the role of memory in the performance of elite athletes? Faced with a decision they must make, an elite athlete—whatever their sport—quickly gives a relevant and reproducible response. In the case of team sports, expertise is not only based on technical skill but also on the ability to make appropriate decisions in a dynamic context where speed is a determining factor. Decision-making is based on comparing the elements emerging from the present situation with the knowledge in the storage memory, called long-term memory; the quantity of information stored and the speed of access to long-term memory are two essential decision-making parameters.

But how do you develop your decision-making? What makes a good or bad decision? How can you decide quickly and well?

What happens when you decide? Neurobiology research shows three stages:

• Your brain searches for other similar decisions in your past to analyze the consequences of those previous decisions.

• Your brain then estimates what you have to gain or lose if you do the action.

• Then, it checks whether the potential gain is worth it, which is to say that it weighs the efforts necessary to achieve it.

In summary, your quick decisions are always what your brain defines as the best-expected result with minimum effort.

So, how do you use this process to make better, faster decisions?

The solution is broken down into three steps:

1. Set a goal for better decision-making.

In a tense situation, your brain will try to maximize its result-to-effort ratio. It will seek the best solution based on emotions, memories, information available, and efforts to provide.

It will have to quickly scan several significant solutions, which will be difficult to compare with each other. It will take time and energy and lead to hesitation, leading to serious errors. But if you know your end goal, your brain can simply consider the solutions available based on your chosen goal. In other words, it can rank them quickly, from the one that best meets your goal to the one that least satisfies it.

So, it's up to you to set your goal.

Warning: "Winning" is not a sufficient objective in the game. How should you win? What is your role in the play? What should you do? Answering these questions is your role. If you have clearly defined it beforehand, your brain, at each decision-making juncture, will be able to refer to your objective to analyze the possible solutions and ask the question, "Does this solution satisfy my objective?"

Knowing your role well means reducing the number of potential solutions and saving time when making decisions.

2.   Foster a quick decision: automate actions.

The "right" decisions must be easy to make quickly. One possible solution is automating the right choices so the brain finds them quickly. Any action consumes energy for the brain, and it will continually seek to minimize the energy expended. This is why it creates automatisms, which consume less energy than sequences constructed voluntarily.

If you want your brain to prioritize an effective solution in an emergency, you should automate it beforehand.

But how do you do this?

Certain situations repeat themselves during the game, or at least can be anticipated. For example, let's say you're caught off guard by the opponent. Instead of panicking and making a hasty decision, plan one or two standard ways to react. They may not be the most effective, but if you find yourself having to respond extremely quickly, they will at least limit the damage and not suffer a bad choice because of the adrenaline rush you are experiencing, which might otherwise cloud your ability to decide.

In general, we repeat certain sequences several times so they become automatic, require less energy to start by the brain, and are started often since the brain sees them as efficient.

To further improve these, it is necessary to judge your results. This requires an analysis of your game:

- Identify the times when you had to make a quick decision.
- What decision did you make?
- Is it consistent with your role/your goal/the game?
- What different decision could you have made?

Do this for bad and good decisions: The goal is to educate your brain by showing what's working well and offering to correct what's going wrong.

By regularly replaying your games, you will improve your automatic reactions and internal communication, gradually achieving a set of efficient and fast automatisms.

Deciding quickly and deciding well comes with practice. It's up to you to put this into practice: play, choose, analyze, correct, and start again.

COGNITIVE DISTORTION AND SENSE OF REALITY

*****

> Magnification: extreme exaggeration of a situation. It intensifies emotions and enhances the loss of lucidity.

The pressures of competitive sports offer ideal situations for creating irrational or distorted cognitive styles. What athletes say to themselves may not positively contribute to success. It may lead to failure. Some athletes and their coaches believe the best performance comes from unconscious thinking (automatic performance). However, expecting an athlete to shut off all cognitive activity while in competition or training is unreasonable. Thinking should not be blamed for reduced performance. Instead, inappropriate or misguided thinking should be the focus of concern.

Four irrational- and distorted thinking beliefs may interfere with athletes reaching their potential. These four beliefs are:

•   I must do well in sports; if I don't, I am incompetent and worthless.

•   I must do well to gain the love and approval of others, and if I don't, it is horrible.

•   Everyone must treat me with respect and fairness at all times.

•   The conditions of my life must be arranged so that I get what I want easily and quickly.

These general beliefs can contribute to athletes' emotional distress and the pressure already present in achievement situations. Distorted thinking styles interfere with performance by providing the athlete with faulty information about the competitive environment, resulting in misdirected attention and emotional distress, such as excessive anxiety and lowered self-concept. Cognitive distortions are thinking errors where poor analytical patterns contaminate your perception of reality. These contribute to the maintenance of negative emotions in decision-making as well as the development of emotional disorders, such as depression and anxiety. The way to counter them is to refute them by questioning them. When you examine them more closely, they will diminish and gradually be replaced by more rational thoughts.

There are a dozen cognitive distortions, of which the main ones are listed below.

- I should

"I should" is often meant to motivate you, but it can have the opposite effect because it contributes to feelings of guilt and inner pressure. When you say "I should," you imply that you must fight or force yourself to convince yourself to take action. Instead of saying "I should," try "I choose ... because I want ..." instead. So, "I should exercise" becomes "I choose to exercise because I want to be in shape." The formula is more flexible and actionable because it defines the objective.

- All or nothing

This distortion is explained by a tendency to categorize your thoughts into extremes without considering any gray area, ignoring the human complexities in between. You will be afflicted by perfectionism and cannot satisfy yourself with the golden mean. So, everything is good or bad, beautiful or ugly, excellent or imperfect.

Strive to move away from black and white, and learn to position yourself in the middle area.

- Generalization

Generalization occurs when you draw a general conclusion based on a single incident. So, based on a single adverse event, you expect it to happen again. Jumping to a general conclusion from a single indication prolongs suffering because, like all or nothing, you are not allowing yourself to see the bigger picture.

- Mental filter

This distortion is explained by the fact that you only remember the negative details of a situation and give them disproportionate attention while forgetting the positive aspects. This element distorts your view of reality.

- Emotional reasoning

This is when you deduce that your feelings reflect reality. You believe what you feel, and by doing this, you lose all objectivity. You take it for granted that your negative emotions are reality. For example, "I feel guilty, so I must have done something wrong," or "I feel embarrassed, so I am incompetent."

- Hasty conclusions

This is your habit of concluding, often harmful, even if no accurate data confirms your interpretation of the situation. For example, you think you know how your friend feels without talking to them, and sometimes you even think you know what they feel about you. This distortion occurs when you interpret others' actions as if you have a crystal ball without bothering to validate your conclusion with them.

- Rejection of the positive

This distortion occurs when you reject all your positive experiences and only consider failures, betrayals, and other adverse events. When you validate a situation based only on negative experiences, you've forgotten nothing good about it. Sometimes, you go even further by turning neutral events into negative ones.

- Perfectionism

This unrealistic expectation leads to excessive pressure, unavoidable failure, and undermining of effective coping. While perfectionism may lead to successful performance, it can destroy athletic careers. It can also lead to negative self-concepts and a fear-of-failure syndrome supported by extreme negative consequences tied to imperfect performance.

- Catastrophizing

Exaggerating potential consequences of imagined or actual adverse events comes along with perfectionism. Those suffering from this distortion expect the worst in every situation—usually worse than reality or previous experience suggests. This can contribute to actual adverse outcomes.

- Self-worth depends upon achievement

Athletes see their self-worth as directly related to their performance and success. This idea mainly concerns young athletes who look to their parents, coaches, and peers for their sense of self. The result is even more stressful performance, low and unstable self-worth, and less fun while participating in sports.

- Personalization

When an athlete employs this distortion, they tend to overestimate their responsibility for every failure and mistake. ("If I only made that last free throw, we would have won the game.") Repeated usage of this type of thinking can result in low self-esteem, high-performance anxiety, and a decrease in the desire to participate and take chances.

- Fallacy of fairness

Fairness often translates into "wanting one's way versus what someone else thinks is fair or best for the group." Unfairness usually results in interpersonal problems, inappropriate focus of attention, and an inability to cope with adversity.

- Blaming

Some athletes excessively attribute failure externally. This gets in the way of improving performance because they never take responsibility for failure.

- Labels

Labels reduce oneself and others into unidimensional terms (e.g., losers, cheaters, unbeatable opponents). They provide a weak mental perspective from which to learn and improve performance.

- One-trial generalizations

Athletes often use a single event to define expectations for future performances. After the first few games of their season, a New York Knicks basketball player was heard to say, "We are a three-quarters basketball team." Such thinking can result in self-defeating prophecy, lack of focus, and lack of attention.

Identifying and modifying irrational and distorted thinking

Identifying these cognitive distortions is the first step toward modifying disturbed thinking styles and enjoying the benefits of rational thinking. Athletes are most teachable immediately following a competition. Coaches should review performance and related thinking, especially after a negative result. Memory fades as time passes.

Coaches often teach athletes distorted thinking styles. Coaches should become aware of their own irrational beliefs and how they model distorted thinking for the athletes.

There are three phases for implementing cognitive restructuring interventions with athletes.

Phase 1: Identification

This step makes us aware when we're experiencing cognitive distortions and helps us know which ones they are. Here are some clues that will tell you that something is up:

You often feel sad and experience negative emotions without clearly identifying the source.

You overreact to situations that concern you.

You tend to belittle yourself and believe others are worth more than you (devaluing).

Your thoughts are negative and easily overflow depending on the topic or event; you ruminate on those thoughts and bring up events you have difficulty accepting.

You harbor resentment toward others and life (envy, idealization).

You believe that you are a victim of events and feel that you can do nothing; you think you haven't had a chance in life, believing that others have more than you (victimization).

To initiate positive change, you must not lie to yourself. Remember, it's always easier to identify other people's problems than our own!

So, if your goal is to correct cognitive distortions, instead of asking yourself why a problem arises, it is more beneficial to know how it is expressed. Focusing on the symptoms will let you know there is a problem and that there is something you can do.

Identification is a process that forces us to take an interest in ourselves, analyze our thoughts and reactions, and understand what is wrong.

This is the first step in eliminating what makes us unhappy. In the identification phase, the boundaries of the affected behavior and the irrational beliefs or self-defeating verbalization present in the situation are defined. Journal writing and conversations can help with the identification.

Phase 2: Questioning

It is not enough to identify cognitive distortion; it must be remedied!

This second step invites us to question our interpretations and our fallacious conclusions.

Deconstruct the problems identified in the first step. First, recover the elements we have identified as the source of our misfortunes. This will allow us to see how our distortions act and, therefore, to end their disastrous consequences consciously.

This questioning underscores the insufficiency of our conclusions and sheds new light on them, which shows us how much they destroy us.

Look for information that may enrich and correct our conclusions, then find new explanations to correct the findings resulting from our distortions. We can come to more nuanced and valid conclusions by taking a fresh look. It's just a matter of finding other ways to interpret our thoughts, negative memories, and situations.

Here are some questions to help you get there:

Interrogate the information on which you are reasoning: "Do I have enough information to conclude? For example, just because I failed to achieve my goal once doesn't mean I will fail every time."

Question your conclusions: "Are my conclusions valid? Do they give me more advantages than disadvantages? Are they realistic? For example, is it constructive to conclude that people who come across these pages of my blog in the future will not find it interesting? If I thought so, I wouldn't be very motivated to continue writing."

Question the beliefs that make you unhappy: "Does the information I have allow me to come to my only conclusion? Are there other possibilities? For example, your coworker may have ignored you because she was preoccupied with a personal problem, not because she finds you insignificant!"

Live happily with more valid beliefs.

Whenever we question the wrong conclusions of our cognitive distortions, we allow ourselves to improve our daily well-being.

Even though these distortions result from our brains' normal functioning, there is no reason to let them poison our existence!

And if happiness does not fall from the sky, we can all distance ourselves from thoughts that destroy our quality of life.

We can devote some effort to straightening our mental posture to live in the happiness we all deserve!

During the questioning phase, the athlete is convinced of the inappropriateness of their thoughts, which leads to more effective thinking. The effectiveness of the intervention depends on getting an athlete to recognize the need to change.

Phase 3: Pairing

In the pairing phase, the athlete uses self-instructional imagery and verbal cues to facilitate the application of new thinking patterns into actual performance. They should practice the imagery several times daily to make the new thoughts automatic. It is essential to emphasize the importance of underlying beliefs in maintaining automatic thoughts. Challenging underlying beliefs is a vehicle for long-term change in thinking patterns.

Purposefully counteracting identified, irrational beliefs is a way of experiencing new thinking and feeling. For example, an athlete who employs excessive criticism and self-abuse after every mistake may try to smile and be overly complimentary after a few mistakes to experience the positive consequences) associated with the new behavior. Athletes and their coaches must try to substitute rational for irrational thinking during all training and competition phases. If athletes have a complicated, irrational belief to rid themselves of, they may benefit from daily affirmation statements that contradict the belief.

Physically relaxing may also increase the effectiveness of attempts to counter irrational beliefs. Most irrational beliefs create anxiety and tension, thus decreasing receptivity to practical, rational thoughts. If doubts exist about whether a belief is illogical or ineffective, ask the following questions: Is the belief based on objective reality? Are they helpful to you? Are they beneficial in reducing interpersonal conflicts? Do they help you reach your goals? Do they minimize emotional strife? If the athlete answers "no" to any of the questions, the belief is likely irrational or counterproductive, and the individual will benefit from modification.

Irrational beliefs are well entrenched in our culture and sports in particular. Examples include "no pain, no gain," "practice makes perfect," and "winning isn't everything; it's the only thing." Many coaches, parents, and athletes believe that modifying some of this type of thinking can lead to less competitiveness. Modifying thinking styles will improve performance because athletes will be more relaxed, focused, and motivated during competition and training.

Consequences of cognitive distortions

Here are some clues that will help you know if you're experiencing cognitive distortions:

Self-denigration: Harsh and inflexible assessments of us that make it seem like we have no personal worth.

Guilt: Wrongly attributing responsibility—inwardly or outwardly—for adverse events.

Victimization: Belief that others often act against us and that we have no control over our lives.

Susceptibility: Feeling that we have no value. This occurs when we doubt ourselves. It hinders our tolerance and interferes with our ability to analyze our behavior and accept mistakes.

Lack of motivation: Convinced of our inability to accomplish anything, we procrastinate, mobilizing neither the energy nor the determination necessary to achieve our goals.

Resentment is the act of rehashing painful past events to relieve them, arousing intense emotions such as sadness and aggression.

Work on the cognitive appraisal to gain lucidity.

Strategic reasoning

"The worst enemy of the strategist is the clock. Time trouble, as we call it in chess, reduces us all to pure reflex and reaction." (Garry Kasparov, former world chess champion).

SECTION 5 DEVELOPING AND ENHANCING LUCIDITY

BUILDING CONFIDENCE

*****

In any sport, confidence is the cornerstone of success and excellence. An athlete who is not confident is undecided, under-motivated, anxious, and does not focus on the stimuli essential to performance.

This type of athlete often has difficulty staying in the present, is not focused on their performance, does not trust their abilities, and overanalyzes themselves. As a result, their muscles are tense, and their actions become hesitant and jerky. Their attention is focused on what not to do instead of what to do. Their fear of failure creates indecision and doubt as their brain fills with technical and strategic thoughts that paralyze them. An athlete lacking confidence is not lucid. They don't use their instincts or trust their training and aren't usually playing in the moment.

It's always easier to be confident when you're playing well, but the challenge is to stay confident even when things aren't going your way, and every athlete struggles with this. Confidence doesn't fall from the sky—it must be acquired and requires a firm commitment. Several strategies exist to improve or regain confidence quickly when lacking.

Two steps to building confidence

1. Analyze your personality

Developing a balanced life requires dedicated introspection. By analyzing each compartment of your life, you will quickly highlight the areas where your ability to control yourself is lacking. Do you have trouble absorbing criticism? Do you fear failure or rejection? By probing your deepest feelings, you will discover why and how to overcome your discomfort. Most people who react aggressively or violently to adversity are oblivious to their weaknesses and ignore the real causes of their behavior. It is crucial to identify the triggers so as not to explode when these feelings arise.

> Remember that knowledge is power. Becoming aware of one's tendency to overreact is already taking the first step toward self-control.

2. Practice self-control

Certain people or situations will always try to destabilize you, but if you identify and rise above them, they'll have less effect on you.

Confidence is precisely this ability to rise above the judgment of others. Only you know who you are and what you want; keep that strength and power of self-control.

Doubting yourself undermines your credibility in the eyes of the world and weakens self-control: How can you keep calm if you constantly consider the judgment of others? To control your emotions, you must not let them invade you and prevent them from dictating your behavior. Self-control involves a long process of understanding and incorporating feelings into your personality. Remember that self-control never comes naturally to us and requires practice and time.

Lack of confidence is a common problem, even among top elite athletes.

In sports, believing in yourself and your possibilities is fundamental. Confidence allows us to dare to take risks, to make choices, and to approach a competition calmly.

Confidence is also significantly involved in learning a new technique or skill in your sport when changing training habits and doing what you know is more straightforward than relearning a new, more efficient method.

Confidence depends on many parameters, including motivation, energy, concentration, and communication, and it is acquired over time.

Where does confidence come from?

- Education (relations with parents, given responsibilities, autonomy)
- Personality (optimist/pessimist, risk-averse/daring, extrovert/introvert)
- Previous life events (such as trauma)
- Previous experiences with failure (how the family responds to failure)
- From other people close to you, such as teammates, coaches, and teachers

The benefits of self-confidence

- Better regulation of behavior and emotions
- Be more persistent
- Look for ways to take on more challenges
- Make more impactful decisions
- Able to focus more on the positive

What can cause a loss of confidence?

- Mistakes and defeats in your sport
- Injuries
- Comparison to others
- Not feeling valued by the people you care about
- Being a constant self-critic
- Not getting enough play time during games

The consequences of a loss of confidence:

- Stress
- Fear of failure
- Inability to accept criticism
- Lack of ambitions
- Concentration on the negative
- Victimization
- Devaluation of skills
- Avoidance, abandonment

Eight ways to improve your self-confidence:

1. Improve your confidence by getting in shape

You may have noticed that your self-confidence can suffer when you're not physically fit.

When physically fit, our technical and tactical mastery level is much better! We feel ready and more positive. Self-confidence is a state of mind directly related to our body, attitude, and thoughts.

Feeling good about your body makes it much easier to feel good in your mind.

2. Think and act with confidence

As we have seen, confidence is directly related to our thoughts and attitudes. More confidence leads to more positive thoughts and better attitudes, and more positive thoughts and attitudes improve confidence. But what can you do if you're not feeling confident?

"Acting as if" means putting yourself in the shoes of a supremely confident athlete. For example, you could have a confident gait, a winning look, positive thoughts, conquering gestures, lots of energy, etc.

3. Be impeccable in preparation for the competition

Being rigorous and conscientious are qualities that champions possess. Before each event, they follow exact routines, which puts them in optimal conditions to approach the competition. It is essential to prepare with intelligence and thoroughness before a competition. This rigor should also be applied to training.

Their pre-match preparation requires a structured approach and a mastery of different parameters:

- Time: Take the time necessary to prepare with serenity
- Routines: Follow clear, precise, simple, and personal routines that allow you to focus on the competition and relieve anxiety
- Warmup: It must be personal, whether in content or in time, and of high quality

- Behavior and thoughts: Learn to orient thoughts to master their pre-competitive period. For example, calm, determined, relaxed, enthusiastic, lucid

By leaving no detail to chance, you will confidently enter the field, and whatever the result, you will have no regrets about your preparation.

4. Improve your self-discipline in training

Training is fundamental for performance. We often hear sayings like "We play as we train" and "Train hard, and you will play easy." Your training and investment quality will usually determine future victories in competition. You may have noticed that your confidence naturally increases when you're good at training. So, give the best of yourself, be focused and involved.

Training is also a special time to become aware of your strengths and weaknesses and to identify attitudes and thoughts that will develop self-confidence.

5. Develop all your mental capacities

As we have seen, confidence is the balance of all parameters. You can increase your confidence by regularly developing different mental skills.

Some examples to work on are goal-setting, motivation, concentration, visualization, energy, emotions, and determination.

6. Use reaffirmations

Whether in training or competition, self-persuasion remains a very powerful technique. You build confidence by mentally or verbally repeating positive words or phrases—whether things are going well or poorly—. For example:

"I am confident in difficult situations."

"I love competition."

"I feel strong."

"I can do it."

7. Watch videos of yourself and great athletes

Watching videos of yourself in action allows you to critique yourself and helps develop self-confidence. Don't hesitate to watch your favorite athletes and teams in action. Observing world-class athletes builds and increases your confidence.

8. Think back to your "top 10"

List your most beautiful athletic actions from a recent or current season. For example:

- The beautiful goals you've scored
- The most technical passes you have made
- The interception or the defensive tackle you made to prevent the opponent from scoring
- Your team's successes.

Write down the 10 best—if you have videos of your actions, it's even better!

Before the match, review your list and relive those good moments in your head. Think back to the pride you felt during these moments, and play them in a loop in your mind. For even more interesting results, you can listen to motivational music simultaneously.

Why do this?

First, it will help you build your confidence, keeping you in a positive, proud state of mind.

Second, viewing your good moves will keep you calm. Because while your mind is busy on the positive sequences, you're not thinking about anything negative.

DEVELOPING EMOTIONAL STABILITY

*****

Being able to control your emotions at critical moments is a skill that separates champions from others. How often have you seen an athlete crumble under pressure during a major competition? Emotional control affects two components: the level of psychological stress and the level of physical intensity. Each athlete is at their best according to a particular relative stress and intensity level. The sport they play also strongly influences the optimal level of intensity. For example, a weightlifter needs a much higher intensity because an explosive force is required. In contrast, that intensity would harm a golfer, who depends more on finesse and coordination.

A high level of intensity, which can be caused by frustration or anger, causes excessive muscle tension and physiological symptoms like a rapid heartbeat, trembling hands, and butterflies in the stomach. Too much muscle tension interferes with the coordination of body movements, resulting in loss of speed and accuracy and fatigue.

Psychological stress, on the other hand, is caused by worry, fear, indecision, and doubt. We must keep stress relatively low to perform at our best. In almost all cases, a high level of psychological stress causes excessive muscle tension, which implies a loss of fluidity and coordination. So, with good stress management, especially under pressure, an athlete can stay focused and perform well.

Reasonable emotional control allows athletes to perform better under pressure and prevents them from losing lucidity and choking.

Knowing yourself well and managing your stress/intensity level is essential to be at your best.

Lucidity in fighting

Lucidity also depends on self-control. After absorbing punishment, many fighters experience pride and nerves overriding the brain, leading to a lack of lucidity. These effects, plus a certain pressure or stress—like the fear of taking a nasty blow—can hinder a fighter's technique.

Lucidity and triathlons

Triathlon transitions often feel like you've slept through the alarm and realized you'll be late for work! These two transitions are key moments in the race. Negotiating them well will not designate you as the event winner, but faltering will cost you a lot of time. At the same time, with a little work organization and lucidity, you will succeed in making quick transitions that will allow you to grab some places.

What is a transition?

These two phases of the race take you from one sport to another: swimming to cycling and cycling to running. Physically, the space is often demarcated and closed, and only athletes and referees can congregate there.

You enter the transition zone before the race to drop off your things. A tiny location is dedicated to you.

Rules govern the transitions:

- You have a traffic direction to respect (so it doesn't look like the Paris ring road at rush hour).
- You cannot ride in the transition zone; you must run alongside your cycle and keep your helmet strapped on your head.

- At the exit, a delimitation on the ground tells you that you can get on your pedals; referees are there to indicate it. Lines and referees are also present at the second transition.

What is happening in your body?

When you start a new sport, you often feel cramps and soreness you'd never felt before. If you think these during a triathlon, it could prevent you from finishing.

Even though you'll mostly use the muscles when you swim, cycle, and run, the environment and your posture will change. Transitioning from swimming (horizontal) to cycling (vertical and seated) can cause cramps, amplified by using your legs very differently in the two sports. Vigorously pumping the legs over the last few meters of the swim is vital since the legs will be called upon abruptly at the exit of the water. You'll need them fully warmed up.

At the second transition, you can mitigate the harmful effects of a change in posture by training. During training, a combined session between two sports should be held once a week. You can, for example, ride 20 to 40 kilometers intensively before immediately running five kilometers. You'll likely experience cramps the first few times, but the more you repeat it, the less frequent the cramps will become. The same will be valid for the swimming-to-cycling transition.

Organize yourself to win minutes.

If you tell yourself that transitions don't matter, you'll lose considerable time on race day. To avoid this, you must be organized. First, before the race, make a checklist of essentials for your transition. Next, place your equipment around your bicycle in a manner that helps you change outfits the fastest. The first important thing is that the saddle spout does the bike placement in 90% of the triathlons; all the bike frames are hung by their saddle and staggered. You will have a handlebar's width to organize your belongings. And during training, you should practice the transition, jogging while beginning to change out of your wetsuit.

Another tip that can save you time during the second transition is to take off your cycling shoes while riding. A few hundred meters before the transition zone, place one foot at the highest point, hold the handlebars with the opposite hand, and unfasten the shoe with your other hand. Repeat for the second shoe. You'll arrive in the transition zone ready to put on your running shoes, and your cycling shoes will remain attached to the pedals.

Finally, on the day of the triathlon, before the start, determine where you'll exit the water and where you'll dismount the bike so as not to become disoriented during the transitions.

SLOW DOWN THE PACE

*****

"Be quick, but don't hurry" (John Wooden, former UCLA basketball coach)

Slowing down your response during pressure reduces your arousal, allowing you to think more flexibly, creatively, and attentively, all forces that help overcome pressure.

To rush comes from the Latin *praecipito*, "to fall head in front."

Whoever rushes reacts without thinking and imposes a form of emergency. They force the course of things and add unnecessary agitation, again pointing to a disruption of action and thought. Whoever rushes has no control over themselves or their environment and simply wants to check something off their to-do list.

Sometimes, in sports, we say we must "hurry slowly." For example, in swimming, the fast swimmer moves quickly while being relaxed, serene, and lucid. The one who rushes is no longer calm, and their emotions are usually in control.

Haste is linked to the emotions that lead us to immediate action, whether fear or anger. We want to eliminate unpleasant tensions by compensatory action, which often aggravates the situation.

Resist the temptation to rush.

Precipitation is the opposite of strategy, anticipation, patience, and reflection. It isn't easy to see anything positive when we're rushing. We jostle and forget things, and it's usually chaotic and involves less thought. It is a sign of nervousness, anxiety, and loss of control. The lone advantage is speed for actions that do not require precision, repetition, or reflection. A tennis player needs to get to the right place at the right time but not in a rush—they should be in control and strike the ball with precision. Rushing is a form of blindness, of automatic action that excludes all thought. We cannot think in haste; we can only react. It is close to panic, which is a total loss of control.

The performance athlete does not rush: their gestures are precise, rapid but not forced, and entirely at one with their environment. We can think here of the archer who strikes their bow with a powerful and rapid gesture but who, at the same time, remains calm and motionless. Any agitation would make them tremble and miss their target. They are both rigid and relaxed. The arrow seems to start from itself; it does not put any will to let go of the rope; it is as if it is the bow that fired all alone. This state of mind of the archer knight is well described in the book Zen in the Art of Archery.

In a badminton match, when you lose a point and have to return the badminton shuttlecock to the opponent, pick it up and keep it until you are ready for the next point. Many players rush to return it, carelessly tossing it back. The opponent may start a new exchange quickly, forcing you to play even when you're not entirely ready. Remember that you dictate the game's rhythm as long as you have the birdie in hand.

Instead of rushing, focus for a few seconds on your breathing and look around at your environment before returning to the game without haste. "You have the right to take your time" is the key permission. This does not prevent you from appreciating your ability to perform specific tasks quickly and efficiently—without rushing!

THE POWER OF INTERMITTENT RECOVERY

*****

Intermittently disengaging is what allows us to reengage passionately.

Eminent sports psychologist Jim Loehr created what he calls the 16-Second Cure. He observed many top tennis professionals and summarized how they manage themselves between points. Loehr used a cognitive behavioral approach, theorizing that behaviors can help shape thinking. By creating a routine, a tennis player can reset themselves regardless of whether the last point was won or lost, difficult or easy.

The 16-Second-Cure includes positive gestures such as pumping a fist or applauding an opponent, a recovery or relaxation phase for deep breathing or muscle relaxation, and a preparation phase for the next point. The order is Respond, Relax/Recover, Prepare, and Play. Loehr realized athletes could not maintain intensity for long, so he created an intensity-rhythm cycle where rest occurs, and maximum effort is saved for the Play phase.

Phase 1: Positive physical response immediately after point ends (duration: 2-3 seconds)

- After a point, show an immediate positive physical response, whether won or lost.
- Carry racquet by throat between thumb and forefinger (do not let racquet droop).
- Project a confident image (shoulders back, head up) so opponents cannot see negativity.

- Walk back into position with high energy.

Phase 2: Relaxation response (duration: at least 10 seconds)

- Turn away from the net.
- Focus eyes not on the court but on strings, ground, or ball.
- Look relaxed and feel loose.
- Take a normal amount of time between shots.
- Walk slowly.

Phase 3: Preparation response (duration: 3-5 seconds)

- Turn around to face the net.
- Raise alertness level.
- Quickly plan out the next point using imagery.
- Use a positive cue or thought to energize, such as "Let's go!"

Phase 4: Ritual (duration: 5 secs)

- Feel confident and know what you want to do.
- Perform deliberate routine whether serving or receiving. For example, the athlete may bounce the ball precisely seven times if serving. If receiving, the athlete may use a fast-feet energizing shuffle to activate the legs before getting into a lower position and sway left and right.

Phase 5: Play (duration: until the point is over)

PRACTICING RELAXATION

*****

Relaxation is an essential key to success in sports. It is to sports what oxygen is to our breathing. It increases and maintains physical efficiency and helps to regain the fluidity necessary for effective gestures. Muscle relaxation allows you to recover the emotional and energetic balance required for performance.

> The real challenge is maintaining relaxation while having an appropriate energy level and alertness.

Relaxation seeks maximum efficiency by contracting the fewest muscles for the shortest period and with the least force.

Muscle relaxation thus reduces energy expenditure unnecessarily generated by tension and parasitic contractions. Efficiency does not just depend on muscle contraction. It also depends on the resistances that oppose it. Thus, the opposing muscles, when tense, counteract the effort exerted.

Mastering relaxation is a long learning process that requires good technical knowledge (what to do) and understanding of your body (what you have to feel). It is a question of consciously seeking relaxation during technical work that requires proprioception (courses, sequences, skill exercises).

Here are some ways to relax muscles: warming up, heat (sauna, shower, bath), deep tissue massages (by another person or by using a foam roller or a lacrosse ball to apply concentrated pressure to a muscle group), stretching (static and dynamic), abdominal breathing (slow and deep), letting go (mental attitude of acceptance), sophrology and Jacobson's progressive relaxation.

How many times have you heard a coach say "relax"? How many times have you told yourself to relax?

Of course, relaxing is easier said than done. But imagine being able to relax on demand.

No muscle relaxation is possible without good psychological availability and emotional management. To be relaxed is to find harmony between body and mind. Followers of yoga, tai chi, and martial arts know this well: they have acquired internal gymnastics, allowing them to relax their bodies consciously.

To find the proper relaxation, we need to reconnect with ourselves and become aware of our bodies—our flesh, breathing, organs, senses, and skeleton.

Our way of life, education, and culture have left us detached from being able to connect to our bodies. At the same time, martial arts enthusiasts inhabit their bellies, allowing them to anchor in the ground and focus on their physical center of gravity, our energetic and emotional center of gravity. It is the most essential part of the human body in martial arts. It is the center from which all techniques arise. On the other hand, in most sports, we are instead focused on the upper part of our body with too many thoughts and emotions— hence our instability and our tension.

Here are three exercises to help with relaxation:

1. Abdominal breathing

To keep your body and mind flexible, abdominal breathing is the most effective exercise to release tension. We habitually breathe through the chest, that is, through the upper lungs. Their respiratory cycle is associated with the alert responses of our body and causes it to be in a state of continual stress. Feelings of anxiety and tension are often associated with it.

On the other hand, controlled breathing through the belly in full consciousness is a natural tranquilizer that brings inner calm, cerebral lucidity, presence of mind, and composure, all of which are precious in our quest for relaxation. Well-controlled breathing contributes to technical optimization and tactical efficiency because we are more lucid and emotionally regulated.

2. Focus on your skeleton

The second exercise focuses on your skeleton for better body awareness because stress does not directly impact our bones. The spine supports all your trunk, arms, head, legs, and pelvis movements. While training, focus on lengthening, proper alignment, and spine flexibility—you'll be amazed by your mobility and gestural fluency. Always focus on your breath throughout the process.

3.   Visualization

The third exercise is a short relaxation through visualization for fifteen minutes an hour before your competition. While breathing through your abdomen, close your eyes and imagine your event with as much detail as possible. Visualize the warmup, your first exchanges with your opponent, and your winning points, and don't forget to see yourself winning the match and shaking hands with your opponent.

As seen in these three exercises, breathing is a constant and essential tool. Be sure to train yourself daily to focus on your breath so that it becomes automatic and the main trigger of your relaxation.

STEPPING BACK

*****

Slow down your thoughts. When we act hastily, our decisions aren't well thought out and aren't usually the right ones.

> Taking a step back is taking the time to question yourself and analyze your thoughts. The result? By putting the situation into perspective, we keep our calm and self-confidence, and above all, we fend off the loss of lucidity.
>
> Under heavy pressure, getting lost in an activity's operational aspects is easy. With your nose in the handlebars, you never take the time to get up and look around. If you're also too emotional, this internal dissociation is particularly difficult. Taking a step back or taking height are techniques that make it possible to gauge a situation from different angles, get out of the spiral of emotion or pressure that submerges us, and regain our power and lucidity.

To move forward, you have to take a step back. Because to step back is to gain momentum.

1. Horizontal way: This is the first and easiest step back level. It's about widening the frame: We zoom out like a camera with a wide-angle lens. Then, the attachment point becomes smaller and fits into a larger whole. This helps us put things in perspective and see the systemic impact of the problem on the immediate environment.

2. Vertical way: This is a way of looking at things from a bird's-eye perspective, like zooming out from a map app on your phone. The point you fix becomes infinitely small as you rise and fit into a large-scale system. It is a good way to cut yourself off from the

emotional feelings that pollute you and become aware of the global whole of which the situation is part.

3. Temporal way: A more elaborate exercise involves recording the point in time on the scale of your life. Has a similar situation already happened? Were there several? Do they form a repetitive pattern, as if you were spinning on a merry-go-round? This allows you to understand the dynamics, to learn from what you have already experienced, and to act to get off the ride permanently.

4. Emotional way: It is the ultimate distance when you are hot-blooded. It's about creating internal dissociation to eliminate polluting emotions. Imagine looking at yourself through a screen. This mechanically cuts off any overflow of emotion.

If you have difficulty keeping your composure, use the emergency technique called "freeze." It consists of your referee telling you to metaphorically inject cooling freon into your emotional powerhouse when you explode. The temperature of the blood drops, you slow down your speech rate and movements, and you ask to take a break. Some people even program a specific alert that they activate on their phone when necessary.

In short, train yourself to soften your vision and to be able to juggle all possible points of view.

TO-DO

1. Activate your internal referee

It is an interior bodyguard responsible for your safety and activating the step-back protocol in various forms. Set it up, give it a face that speaks to you (a film character, a loved one, even an animal), and officially instruct it to help you in difficult situations, to "wake you up" when you lose composure and lucidity.

2.   Exercise regularly

Start by training to step back, gain height, and function with your internal referee in medium-difficulty situations. Then, when you reach the autopilot stage, try it with more complex situations. Like all mastery, self-control is the result of intense practice.

3. Take back the power

Tell yourself that your inner self belongs to you and that the emotions that inhabit it, no matter how strong, are under your control. It is necessary to clean it regularly. To do this, the recipe is simple: distance yourself from the negative (emotions, elements), relativize it by gaining height and perspective, and, on the contrary, maximize and focus on the positive by zooming in on it.

REACHING A STATE OF DETACHMENT THROUGH HYPNOSIS

*****

From the willingness to let go…to letting go…to hypnosis.

What is hypnosis?

Hypnosis is a modified state of consciousness.

Our thinking is simple: Hypnosis professionals can help people overcome phobias, gain self-confidence, learn more quickly, eliminate depression, or sleep better. They can also help an athlete be calm before a competition and concentrate on whatever the conditions of play are while optimizing movements, improving training, and speeding up recovery.

> Hypnosis is a natural state of consciousness like reverie or concentration. To access it, you must learn to modify your usual state and control this modification like a fine-tuned machine. For example, a state of peak performance means moving with precision, grace, and a feeling of effortlessness. It is a surreal state that makes the athlete feel like they view themselves from a spectator's perspective.

Athletes already experience some states of hypnosis regularly without realizing it. The extremely fast pace of specific sports, the intensity or the length of a race, and the level of fatigue are among the ingredients that sometimes spontaneously lead to altered states of consciousness.

These states are often perceived as mindful presence, excellent fluidity, and high performance. They are perceived as states of grace in which everything happens like a dream. An athlete who experiences them feels like a spectator watching and enjoys the freedom to act with precision. You have probably experienced these states, and unfortunately, as you may have noticed, they quickly dissipate when the mind tries to control them and take over. How do you maintain this hypnotic state of being?

The mastery of maintaining that state requires training.

How did you learn to walk, write, speak? These skills are now part of you and deeply rooted; they do not depend on you anymore. You can't look at a word and not read it. Our unconscious mechanisms go faster than the conscious ones, and all of this is fully automated. Once something becomes automated, our consciousness has no say or control. These skills become natural reflexes when they pass the stage of voluntary control.

Our most profound skills—those that have become reflexes— have been integrated at an unconscious level beyond the will of consciousness. This is a natural, logical process. If we seek to do so through the will, we block this process.

Take the example of sleep. People who have experienced insomnia have experienced a moment in which they consciously wanted to sleep. We have all known how to fall asleep since birth, but we do not know how to fall asleep consciously. Wanting to sleep almost always results in sleeplessness. Too much willingness blocks our natural processes and stops our unconscious reactions.

On the contrary, letting go allows us to fall asleep. By relaxing, we also allow our unconscious processes to act more freely.

But simply letting go is not very effective. Daydreaming is not enough to learn and integrate perfectly, and too much inattention hurts learning, as we can easily imagine. Daydreaming is a state of mindlessness.

The ideal state combines a particular form of conscious presence with a retreat or relaxation that allows the most unconscious part to synthesize information in us and absorb it.

We seek a mindful state that focuses on a goal, allowing us to learn without stimulating our will too intensely. We are looking for a state that allows us to be absorbed by an action, losing track of time with intense focus, creativity, and innovative ways to do things without trying to control our state.

The hypnotic state is not about being close to sleep. It is a state of alternative, modified consciousness. This state stimulates certain brain functions and allows information from a lived experience to be processed unconsciously.

Thus, a person under hypnosis memorizes better, has improved reflexes, and can act on deep learning to modify their reflexes. This technique has been used for centuries in therapy. Hypnosis explores thoughts, feelings, and memories that may have been hidden from the conscious mind. It can also be used to improve self-confidence, diminish pain, relieve anxiety, enhance relationships, improve health, quit smoking, assist in weight loss, and support healing from trauma. It works for many forms of personal work and change.

Hypnosis allows us to go beyond the conscious/unconscious border to reach deeper parts of ourselves, escape, act on our emotions, and program or reprogram our reactions, gestures, and behaviors.

Failing to act on your unconscious is like leaving some of your potential in a wild state. Hypnosis makes it possible to channel, tame, and shape emotions. This transformation allows emotions to reach a desired objective or dream. It is an essential tool for someone who wants to move forward and pursue their most fabulous self.

Once these bases are laid, we can move into a more practical dimension.

Alternate perception: associate/disassociate

There are two positions within which everyone lives: the associated position and the dissociated position.

When overcome with emotion, we often blush, smile, and have multiple physical reactions. If the body reacts to the feeling, it is an associative experience. In other words, our physical response is associated with the emotional experience. Conversely, being dissociated means remaining "cold" (no facial expressions or gestures)—at least on the surface at a precise moment—and being self-observant, with a more analytical attitude.

One position is not better than another. The position may change based on the circumstances. It is the alternation from one state to the other that interests us. It's easy to imagine that if we needed surgery, we would prefer that it be done by a surgeon who was a master of his emotions (dissociated) rather than by a hyper-associated surgeon who would be overwhelmed by the slightest unforeseen event. After being dissociated from his work, this same surgeon will return home and undoubtedly reassociate to play, laugh, and share good moments with his family. This is just one of many examples.

Some professions require association. For example, retail sales clerks, communication specialists, actors, and grade-school teachers must be highly associated to perform their jobs. On the other hand, pilots, CEOs, safety professionals, accountants, and military servicepeople rely on a dissociated state to remain coolheaded and logical. These are generalities, but the critical idea is that we have these two types of perceptions about our experiences.

We have them mentally, too. The principles of association and dissociation can be understood by answering the following question: When you think of a good moment during competition, do you see the scene like a film, or are you reliving it through your own eyes, as if you were there again?

Making a small effort to move from one position to another mentally creates a modified state of consciousness and induces hypnosis.

The hypnosis technique.

Make a conscious effort to dedicate your undivided attention to refocusing yourself.

1. The first step is association. Concentrate on your breathing while you sit with your eyes closed and mentally scan the feelings of the body from the bottom up.

2. The next step is dissociation. Imagine moving forward from a sitting position, leaving a double of yourself behind you. Now imagine turning around to look back at your double. In this dissociated position, you can see how that person breathes, how their body moves, and how they have facial expressions. Notice which muscles of their body are relaxed and which remain slightly contracted. As you're watching your double, you enter a state of hypnosis. Observing from the outside makes your body seem distant and your feelings less intense.

3. Approach your double to the point of fusing with them and feel what they are experiencing. Explore the state that has deepened within them and the new sensations that have appeared. Now imagine that you're returning to being inside the double you initially imagined. After being severely dissociated, this should seem strange,

and you should be particularly receptive and sensitive to your feelings. The new associated position creates a hyper-presence, a sensation of physical intensity. You must raise your concentration level until you feel aware of every detail of your body before you dissociate again.

4. For the second dissociation, imagine that you move forward for a second time, leaving a double of yourself sitting behind you. This time, move forward a little farther than before; imagine the space between you and the double growing. Then turn around and watch, as in step 2, as your double continues to deepen their state of hypnosis.

5. For your mind to accept that these two positions are different, it will require several trips of progressively increasing the space between you and the double. This will require experimentation, but four to five visits should be enough.

6. After these round trips, make the following suggestion: "Now I'm coming out of the state of hypnosis." Reassociate yourself with the one sitting on the chair, who is now waking up. As you go through the association process, you will also emerge from hypnosis and wake up because this person is you.

For some people, the choice between the two positions is not apparent. Those who say, "I cannot show my emotions" or "I am too emotional" have only one of two possibilities. In a way, this technique is a form of mental reeducation.

Moreover, the dissociated position is more objective and analytical than the associated position, which is more reactive and emotional. The athlete's ability to switch between positions is a valuable asset.

By nature, the dissociated position cuts sensations from the body. Moving farther away and being slightly more withdrawn is helpful in some situations. This can create a form of hypnotic anesthesia (inability to feel pain without the loss of consciousness) or spontaneous analgesia (which, in certain circumstances of the athlete's life, may be helpful).

The exercise is successful when you dissociate enough to have the impression of forgetting your body or when you are associated with the point of experiencing a strong hypersensitivity.

The eye of the tiger.

Most of the time, we use a centrally focused vision. Our attention requires precision, and our eyes must follow. However, we have retained some archaic reflexes and another kind of vision: peripheral. For example, the martial arts fighter observes all their opponent's movements while focusing on their opponent's face. They do not need to move their head to look down; they use their peripheral vision to focus on what matters most, and they can react to the things that come along their path.

Like the previous technique, moving from one vision style to another will shift consciousness. Sensory absorption and concentration will be activated more intensely. Endurance athletes will no doubt recognize similarities between this state and their athletic experiences.

The technique.

1. Adopt the sitting or standing position that is most pleasant for you. Focus on a point or object in front of you at eye level. Once your eyes are fixed, you can continue to blink to keep the technique comfortable.

2. After about a minute, distinguish between your visual awareness and the position of your eyes. Notice that they are distinct from each other.

3. Without moving your eyes, expand your visual awareness—for example, to the left and right of the point on which your gaze is fixed.

4. Without your gaze leaving the focus point, defocus your attention from this point and direct it toward your peripheral visual space.

5. Enlarge your attentional field by listening to your surroundings.

6. You will experience several things. The first is a natural slowing of your thoughts. The second is a more distant awareness of your body. The third may be modifying your vision (but not hallucinations).

7. To get out of this state of hypnosis, start by thinking, "In a few moments, this state will disappear, and I will return completely well to the present moment." Observe how your body reacts and when your vision becomes more regular.

One significant advantage of this technique is that it can be practiced with open eyes. It allows you to slow down and stop your thoughts. In addition, it creates a form of dissociation from the body, in which feelings of fatigue and pain seem to diminish.

This discreet technique can be practiced while motionless, sitting, standing, walking, running, or swimming. It's like a Swiss army knife that can control your thinking in moments of action during which all your concentration is needed. It is also an invisible gateway to the state of self-hypnosis. However, this exercise may be more effective if a partner walks you through the process since it requires you to be patient with yourself as you learn the techniques.

LEARNING HOW TO ANTICIPATE

*****

How can you develop anticipation in your sport? Be one step ahead, and be prepared for the unexpected.

Combat sports illustrate very well the importance of anticipation.

Anticipation requires patience and a calm mind and can be done at two levels. The beginner level consists of intercepting the attack when the opponent's body initiates its movement. The expert level consists of intercepting the attack during the opponent's decision-making before initiating the movement. To do this, you must develop your intuition.

The anticipation of the emotional and intellectual

Anticipation must be done in a way that depends on the opponent, either emotionally or intellectually. Each fighter has a proportion of emotionality and intellectuality in them. The fighter will have specific characteristics depending on which of the two is predominant.

The anticipation of an intellectual fighter is more with the mind, while the anticipation of the emotional is more with the heart.

Those who do the action with their heart can grasp it quickly because of intense emotion. The raw intention is then easier to feel. The intellect will be more challenging because it works less in emotion. It will then have to be analyzed more rationally.

The feeling of the other

To anticipate, you must get a deep sense of the opponent. The better you grasp the opponent in their most profound nature, the more you can control them. We must try to capture our emotions, thoughts, fears, moments of hesitation, and doubt. One should try to detect one's strengths and weaknesses, both physical and mental.

We can successfully detect the moment of decision-making of the action by listening to our interior. We can feel deeply, in our bowels, the opponent's intentions. This vital biological faculty has been part of our defense mechanisms since birth. All living things can sense danger thanks to an internal radar that sounds the alarm and activates our body to trigger an immediate defense response. With the time and the quiet life that we lead, safe from dangers, we have put this vital faculty to sleep.

Exercise: Stand with your eyes closed, facing a partner who will attack you with great intensity and conviction. Try to feel the moment when the partner will initiate their action. By listening deeply to yourself, you can feel the moment they decide to launch their attack before they even move. To get there, it takes mental calm and great concentration. Then, the challenge is to reproduce this feeling in combat with your eyes open.

This openness to others requires a lot of listening. We must also pay our full attention to the opponent. Beginners tend to think for themselves: What technique will I use next? What is my coach telling me? What will happen if I lose? However, attention should be focused exclusively on the opponent. You have to be one with the other to feel your emotions and your intentions. This union with the other allows understanding of rhythm and makes intuition finer.

"You are one with your opponent. There is a coexistence relationship between you. You coexist with your opponent, become their complement, absorb their attack, and use their force to control them. —Bruce Lee

To respond adequately to the attack, you must enter the rhythm and distance used by the opponent. These notions must be felt and learned from the first seconds of the fight.

Stabilize body and mind for anticipation.

> To succeed in anticipation, the body and mind must always be available.

Spirit available: You have to be able to maintain a conception of intense input throughout the fight. Each flaw becomes an opportunity for the opponent. The mind must be free, detached, focused, and ready to react to any situation.

Body available: During movement, the body must always be able to protect itself or to attack. To do this, the limbs and the body must be well positioned. It is necessary to practice making movements in stable and malleable positions with flexible and rapid transitions, always having the guard well placed.

In karate, sakki is the feeling of the attack coming.

Anticipation tightens the pace of the fight and makes it more subtle. Stopping and blocking are defensive attacks that rely entirely on anticipation. Likewise, dodging, withdrawals, and displacements are often caused by predicting the coup's trajectory or the opponent's intentions.

The phenomenon of anticipation remains mysterious. We can speak of telepathy or intuition, which goes beyond the simple analysis of manifest signs in the opponent. But since telepathy and intuition are mysterious phenomena, they do little to help us understand anticipation.

We have studied the mechanisms that allow the brain to calculate the trajectory of a ball thrown by an opponent (in tennis, in particular). It was determined that the brain only considers the start of the ball to get an idea of its general trajectory and the arrival of the ball to correct the first idea. The brain does not analyze the intermediate trajectory.

In the case of a strike, the brain knows perfectly well the movements that an arm or a leg can perform. Observing even the slightest sketch of the opponent's maneuver seems sufficient to anticipate the entire move, especially with great experience.

Is the ball on target? What will my opponent do? A football goalkeeper does not wait for the ball to be in the net before diving toward it; a boxer who doesn't read their opponent's punches until they have landed wouldn't be very successful.

Perceptual anticipation is an essential skill in most sports. Beyond these examples, predicting the movements of objects and people around us is a key function of our visual perception. We are in an environment in perpetual movement, either because the elements composing it move or because we move. Consequently, the cognitive system faces a significant challenge: the time necessary to process visual information, from the image on the retina to the analysis of the scene by the brain, means that when we see the world, it changes. However, when we catch a falling object, we place our hand where the object is and not where it was when its image hit our retina.

Thanks to the cognitive mechanisms of perceptual anticipation, we see the environment as it will be rather than as it is. These mechanisms evolve with the development and acquisition of expertise, such as in sports.

We are constantly projecting ourselves into what we will see the next second. What are the cognitive processes responsible for this phenomenon? Do we have a common anticipation mechanism that allows us to extend the movement of any object, or are there mechanisms specific to each domain? According to this second hypothesis, we would not anticipate the movement of a car using the exact mechanisms as those allowing us to predict a balloon's trajectory.

Several experiences support this second point: anticipation depends on the knowledge we have acquired in a field. Acquiring expertise improves anticipation skills. The hours and years spent in the field increase understanding of the sport, and their database allows the player to predict in a short time what will happen during an action. This rapid phenomenon is automatic, adapts to situations, and undoubtedly represents the key to success in activities where anticipation is crucial, such as team sports. As a result, we have cognitive mechanisms, which, without our knowledge, use our past experiences to anticipate what will happen. The more we become experts in a field, the more these mechanisms refine. Athletes are the best example of this: A professional basketball player could receive a pass from a teammate even if the stadium's spotlights went out just after the pass had been released.

DEVELOPING YOUR INTUITION

*****

What is intuition?

When we trust our intuition, our brain calls upon memories we're unaware of to give us an orientation or a choice without knowing precisely why. Intuition is in the right hemisphere. It comes from analogies, representations, perceptions, and images. Intuition results from our capacity to process a large number of information recorded in each person's unconscious, which is the fruit of experiences, reflections, and meetings.

Intuition is also the result of a process and not, as collective agreements want us to believe, a vision, something that would come under mysticism or divination. For example, when our intuition tells us that a person is not safe, there is a high probability that we have already faced similar situations. The right hemisphere, where intuition resides, considers things as a whole, while the left brain sorts and classifies but can immediately perceive what it is about from a detail. In a fraction of a second, it perceives a person's direct and instant apprehension of all things. The left brain must then translate their perception of reality as a whole. Intuition can be defined as immediate knowledge of a reality presently in mind.

For philosopher René Descartes, intuition and logical deduction complement each other.

For neuroscientists, intuition is a form of intelligence that everyone has. The rational part of our brain manages our learning, and the more emotional, relational, and adaptive part allows us to get out of repetitive logical constraints. Intuition would have to do with this ability to imagine predictable, illogical responses and solutions.

There is no limit to trusting your intuition if you know the difference between intuition and desire. Intuition is only what one has unconsciously analyzed. Intuition is beneficial for everyone, and it can be worked on and developed. It is a colossal compass that allows you to shape your daily life as closely as possible to your needs, desires, and athletic skills. Undoubtedly linked to self-confidence, you still have to trust yourself.

The prefrontal cortex would automatically assimilate the multiple parameters involved and deliver a solution through intuition or instinct. In self-defense, should you trust your instinct or your intuition? Which one should you listen to? The two are inseparable and have an essential role anyway.

And what is intuition not?

It seems easier to say what intuition is not than what it is. Contrary to popular belief, intuition is not the product of our emotions. Intuitive intelligence is not emotional intelligence. On the contrary, emotions would prevent us from listening to our intuition. For example, we are often blinded and reluctant to listen to our inner voice when feeling fear or anger.

Likewise, intuition has nothing to do with opinion, judgment, or prejudice. If a person makes a bad impression because they have a style that you don't like, it's not intuition.

And neither is it desire. If you have a great desire to go to Europe and when you see an advertisement for flights to Paris, you feel pushed to buy, it is not intuition. You're simply reacting to a desire.

Accurate intuition is emotionally neutral. It is often unexpected, even unexplained, and manifests through bodily sensations, sudden ideas, or impressions. But then, where does it come from?

Where does intuition come from?

Behavioral sciences are very interested in intuition. However, we have not succeeded in explaining or locating the mechanisms that give rise to intuitive feelings.

We have two modes of mental functioning: an automatic mental mode, which integrates our routines, and a prefrontal mental mode, which analyzes and can adapt to newness. Most of the time, we are connected by default to automatic mode. Creative intuition is the signal that indicates to our prefrontal mental mode that we must readjust our conduct.

Does intuition come from the unconscious or elsewhere?

Because it does not come from our conscious thought, psychologists hypothesize that intuition is a message from our unconscious. Intuition would help us untie buried emotional knots.

But how can we explain then that the children, who have very little past, are so intuitive?

For them, like many great thinkers, intuition is not necessarily explained in the past. It would come from elsewhere, from another dimension of being, reality, or the cosmos.

What is an intuition for?

Let's say you are welcomed into a new village, and at some point, you intuitively sense a change of atmosphere, and you know that you need to leave in an emergency.

Intuition often allows you to be in the right place at the right time, usually called luck.

In more ordinary situations, better listening to your intuition can save you time, blockages, and unnecessary detours while guiding you to the right solutions, especially those with whom you will work well.

In the longer term, intuition helps us determine which direction to orient our lives to align with our deep personality.

Why don't we trust intuition?

We don't listen to it mainly because we can't explain it, and it primarily appeals to the unconscious. The unconscious mind accounts for 90 percent of the human brain's activity. It is where all the most profound memories, thoughts, and emotions are stored. In today's rational and logical reasoning world, intuition has always been looked down upon.

Seen and designated as an inexplicable feeling or sensation, impossible to prove through logic or scientific demonstration, it was considered unreliable and close to esotericism. However, intuition is taking advantage of one's baggage by instinctively using reasoning through analogy. Our brain constantly processes data, eliminates what is incidental, and allows us to draw the necessary conclusions instantly.

How to listen to your intuition?

All of this ultimately makes you want to listen to your intuition better, especially since the good news is that we can all do it.

Intuition is not a gift that some would have found in their cradle at birth and others would not. It also has nothing magical and is not particularly feminine, as in the phrase "women's intuition."

We all have intuition, but some people know better how to recognize it and have gotten into the habit of considering it. They are attentive to the small signals by which their intuition manifests itself, and above all, they manage to put aside their need for rationality. Finally, they know how to trust themselves!

It is enough to progress on these points to be more intuitive, and we can all do it.

How can you get better at listening to intuition?

To better listen to your intuition, you can:

- Tell your mind to stop. Our need for rationality is the main obstacle to listening to our intuition. Faced with intuition, you should not want to find evidence to reassure yourself (since intuition does not provide evidence) but trust your feelings.

- Learn to recognize intuition. Intuition is never accompanied by fear or the fruit of our judgments. Another clue: It is often the first message to reach us in a given situation. Intuition always comes first. When we experience a new problem, we must be attentive to this first intuitive feeling and remain faithful to the information, whatever our resistance, fears, and doubts.

- Practice your sport regularly: This makes you more attentive to physical sensations and ideas that arise without coming from the mind. Thus, we are better at letting go and feeling in a different way than through rational thoughts. In competitive sports, you must be able to analyze a situation or an opponent to anticipate and act.

- Be in the present moment. Intuition is experienced in the present. If our mind ruminates on memories or anticipation, it will miss the passage of intuition. We can practice relaxation and meditation to refocus on the here and now.

- Break away from the obligation of a result. A good idea often springs up when you stop looking for a result. We find the concept of relaxation and letting go.

- Trust yourself. Get into the habit of seeing your talents, successes, and strengths, and tell yourself that you are the only person who can listen to your insights because you are unique.

But isn't there also bad intuition?

Instinct

In self-defense, what differentiates intuition from instinct? Trusting your instinct or intuition in self-defense is listening to all your senses and being aware of your environment.

The human brain is divided into two hemispheres with different functions.

The left hemisphere controls the right part of the body and is analytically oriented for language, calculations, writing, logic of reasoning, and intelligence. It is programmable and consolidated by our analytical education. The left hemisphere is very attached to time, rules, and facts. With our left brain, we reason sequentially, analytically, and point-by-point.

The right hemisphere controls the movements of the left part of the body. Its functions are unique because they are not sequential, such as visual perception, instinct, or intuition. This half of the brain also records all nonverbal communication. The right hemisphere stores knowledge and processes large amounts of information.

What is instinct?

Instinct is the reptilian brain. It allows us to make decisions about our survival. We often think that the survival instinct is linked to emotions. Nature has given all animals the instinct for self-preservation. Instinct is an internal movement natural to animals that makes them act without the recourse of reflection to perform acts in accordance with their species and adapt to their needs. Each species has its instinct.

But instinct appeals a lot to emotion, and emotion can make decisions that are sometimes entirely absurd., In this case, this will push humans to adopt inconsiderate or disproportionate behaviors.

Following your instincts in self-defense in situations of great stress is beneficial. Still, you must be careful not to let emotions overwhelm you and interfere with rational thinking.

CONCLUSION

Lucidity: reaching a modified state of consciousness

To reach the best performance, the athlete must enter a mental state that allows them to have extreme physical presence to create precise movement and flawless control. This is only possible when they have extreme lucidity about themselves and the world.

Almost all champions felt that unique, optimal state of concentration while remaining open to the information necessary to conduct the action. Laura Flessel, fencing champion, and multiple Olympic medalist, expresses this analysis clearly:

"Whenever I feel in this state, I have my feet on the ground and am clear-headed."

Mindfulness is a healing technique inspired by Buddhism and yoga created in the 1970s by biologist Jon Kabat Zinn. Indeed, this technique is used to reduce stress and prevent depressive relapses. The principles of mindfulness also apply to athletes wishing to improve their attentional capacity, emotional management, and lucidity.

Mindfulness is a focus of one's attentional field on the whole of the personal experience of the moment (breathing, heartbeat, sensory perceptions, thoughts, etc.), adopting a nonjudgmental attitude toward the current experience. This altered state of consciousness translates into living in the present moment without trying to analyze or put into words what we're experiencing. It's just about welcoming what comes in the moment.

Many athletes describe signs of stress linked to a competitive situation: sweaty hands, a faster heartbeat, a knotted stomach, and heavy legs. These physiological signs are typical when the stakes are higher, and adrenaline is distilled in the body.

When you come out on the pitch before an important game or have to finalize an action, are your thoughts focused on the present moment? Are you in complete control of your means? Or are you flooded with stray thoughts, doubts, and questions?

If your mind is only concerned with performance and results, it affects your lucidity and decision-making. Mindfulness helps in this sense.

When a person practices this technique, several brain areas are stimulated. Neuroscience research highlights the increase in brain activities involved in engagement and attention (visual cortex), its maintenance (dorsolateral prefrontal cortex), and its orientation (intraparietal and superior frontal grooves). Expert meditation practitioners also show less amygdala activation, allowing them to free themselves from their emotional reactions.

Several techniques exist, though the ones used most often involve paying close attention to what is happening in and around you. Whether the sensations are pleasant or unpleasant, the idea is to adopt an attitude of curiosity by observing in a detached manner without seeking control, all while having minimal emotions and thoughts.

It's like a skier sliding in powder snow hugging the slope's contours or a surfer following the movement of the waves without trying to change them. The more we try to control our thoughts, the more it can tend to exacerbate them. Conversely, trying not to think induces belief.

Practicing this type of meditation teaches you not to get fixated or stuck on any thought, sensation, or perception. Thus, thoughts are less captive to what could distract them from their goal.

Concretely, before beginning an exercise they don't feel confident about, a gymnast would say to themselves, "On the bars, I always feel weaker. I must not miss it. And I have to stop thinking." They will then likely feel stress related to the situation and their thoughts. If they remain focused on this thought, they are no longer in the present moment, and they risk a worse performance than if they could, in full consciousness, accept this apprehension and focus on the way of doing things. A tennis player with a double fault may stay focused on that mistake rather than the point they're playing. Instead of being in the present moment, they think about the past, which they no longer control. Mindfulness would help keep them from fighting with their thoughts, making them lose energy. The real fight is on the ground.

Many athletes feel stress, nervousness, and impatience and are not always confident in competitions and games. They are good at training but cannot play at the same level in games despite knowing they have the potential.

Imagine a rugby player in the World Cup Final. All they need to do to fulfill their dream is to convert the penalty in the last seconds of the match. It's something they've done so many times in their career.

But that day, there were other thoughts on that penalty, like "I mustn't miss it." They notice the crowd and the scoreboard and think about how many people count on them to perform this gesture correctly and win the tournament. They think of everyone who expects a lot from them, including themselves.

So, this penalty is not quite the same as all those made so far. This player prepares to shoot like all the other times by putting the ball down, doing his routine, and finally kicking the ball. Then the unthinkable and unexpected happens: he cracks under pressure and misses, and his team loses the tournament.

"Choking" is often used in sports circles to describe an unexpected drop in performance in anxiety-provoking situations. Such situations can be encountered in the presence of an audience, by the possibility of great reward if one succeeds, by competition, or by factors unique to the individual.

The athlete will tend to feel anxiety, and to cope with it, they will invest more in the task, which can hurt performance because their attention may no longer be focused on the relevant points of it.

Mindfulness helps promote anchoring, and the presence of the mind is essential for remaining calm. It prevents thoughts from wandering and straying.

What matters is how you respond in the present moment.

This is the mission. Find a way to shape your inner world— your mind, so to speak—and organize your inner life to find yourself present where you are in any setting, situation, and circumstance. If you can do this, the results will happen on their own.

ACKNOWLEDGMENTS

*****

Stephanie Cunha and Lisa Lucchesi, thank you for reading this book. We genuinely hope you can use a concept from this work to help you in your athletic development and life. We want to thank all our contributors, collaborators, and clients at Mental Accelerator. We are grateful for the opportunity to serve you each day.

ABOUT THE AUTHORS

*****

STEPHANIE CUNHA is a biochemist and entrepreneur in the mental strength training industry.

While being a competitive athlete and winning the mountain biking cross-country Rhone-Alpes trophy cup in 2007 and 2008, she obtained 2008 her PhD in Molecular and Cellular Biology and Biochemistry at the prestigious University of Lyon 1 in France.

Passionate about the function of the body's molecules on the brain and emotions, she pursued her research in sports psychology and developed practical tools for athletes to optimize their mindset, which would later become the Adaptive Mindset System ™.

Stephanie moved to the USA in 2009 to complete her postdoctoral fellowship at the University of Utah. While having the best mountain biking experience and playing soccer in Salt Lake City, she will pursue her research and spread the Adaptive Mindset System among the mountain biker and soccer communities. During these years, she became a member of the American College of Sports Medicine (ACSM) and was elected as an evidence analyst. In 2015, Stephanie became an ACSM certified trainer. The following year, she moved to Portland, Oregon, where she started to practice

Shotokan Karate and met Lisa Lucchesi, a chemist and a leader at Nike.

LISA LUCCHESI is a leader at Nike in all things related to testing, with a motto of "You make it, she breaks it." Before working at Nike, she was a product developer for 15 years in the medical device industry, taking products from concept, scale-up, and tech transfer through commercialization. Her pet projects included wound dressings for severe bleeding for the military, which received the second-fastest FDA approval and were awarded status among the top 10 greatest Army inventions of 2004.

Her expertise is developing fast, effective, and relevant strategies for iterative product improvements, sports, and life improvements.

Her motivators are family, developing others, and learning. She is very in tune with others' emotions and inspired to help others reach their full potential, and she thrives on trying new systems and growing. In sports, like business and research, many obstacles stand in the way of getting to the next level. She is ready to share her learning to help the athletic community overcome these challenges.

She struggled with mental health challenges throughout her life, and sports played a critical role in helping her achieve a strong mindset. She played softball for seven years as a preteen through high school and was an avid mountain biker for five years. In March 2020, she obtained her second-degree black belt in Shotokan karate.

Stephanie Cunha and Lisa Lucchesi founded Mental Accelerator in 2019. It is a professional coaching service that offers products and training programs for athletes.

MAXIMUM
COMPOSURE

DOMINATE EMOTIONS WITH
THE ADAPTIVE MINDSET SYSTEM™

STEPHANIE CUNHA, Ph.D.
LISA D LUCCHESI, M.S.

For more content on the athlete's mindset, visit us at:

www.MentalAccelerator.com

www.ingramcontent.com/pod-product-compliance
Lightning Source LLC
LaVergne TN
LVHW011226080426
835509LV00005B/334